flat out rock

TEN
GREAT BANDS
OF THE '60s

MIKE TANNER

annick press
toronto + new york + vancouver

Annick Press Ltd.

We acknowledge the support of the Canada Council for the Arts, the Ontario Arts Council, the Government of Canada through the Book Publishing Industry Development Program (BPIDP) and the Ontario Book Publishing Tax Credit (OBPTC) for our publishing activities.

Edited by Antonia Banyard
Copyedited by Derek Fairbridge
Proofread by Derek Fairbridge and Melissa Edwards
Photo research by Antonia Banyard
Cover and interior design by Irvin Cheung/iCheung Design

The publisher wishes to acknowledge Ross Macnab, Asia McLean, and Zevon Feen for unwittingly inspiring the idea for this book. May you continue to rock.

Cataloguing in Publication
Tanner, Mike, 1960 –
    Flat-out rock: ten great bands of the '60s / by Mike Tanner.

Includes bibliographical references and index. ISBN-13: 978-1-55451-036-8 (bound) ISBN-10: 1-55451-036-8 (bound) ISBN-13: 978-1-55451-035-1 (pbk) ISBN-10: 1-55451-035-X (pbk)

    1. Rock music—1961-1970—Juvenile literature. 2. Rock groups—Juvenile literature. 3.Rock musicians—Biography—Juvenile literature. I. Title.
ML394.T167 2006   j781.66'092209046   C2006-901206-7

Printed and bound in China

Published in the USA by	**Distributed in Canada by**	**Distributed in the USA by**
Annick Press (US) Ltd.	Firefly Books Ltd.	Firefly Books (US) Inc.
	66 Leek Crescent	P.O. Box 1338
	Richmond Hill, ON	Ellicott Station
	L4B 1H1	Buffalo, NY 14205

Visit our website at **www.annickpress.com**

Introduction

The bands and individual artists in this book are unique musical talents. They differ widely from each other when it comes to their style and their songs—but they also have much in common. Let's take a closer look.

First, all of these musicians created sounds that had never been heard before. Whether it was the folk-rock of Bob Dylan, the swamp rock of Creedence Clearwater Revival, or the hard rock of Led Zeppelin, a musical revolution took place in each case. Every musician used what had come before and added something personal to break new ground. Each band, singer, player, and songwriter also kept moving forward. Not one was content to remain in the same place, musically speaking, for long.

Second, the artists in this book brought a special passion and energy to music. No audience had witnessed total power unleashed onstage until the Who let loose in London's clubs during the mid-'60s. Never had a white woman sung gut-wrenching blues like Janis Joplin did when she knocked the crowd out at the Monterey Pop Festival in 1967.

Third, all the musicians you'll read about here caused their share of controversy. Dylan and Neil Young did it just through the songs they wrote. Others, such as the Rolling Stones and the Doors, made waves

US President Kennedy formed the Peace Corps in 1961 as a way to involve the nation's youth in the cause of spreading democracy around the world. Thousands of university graduates, idealistic and eager for adventure, signed up.

partly because of the lives they led offstage, and how their dangerous images affected the music they created.

Finally, nobody in these pages cared as much about pleasing the accountants or the critics as they did about artistic honesty. If an album sold millions, that was great—as long as the songs expressed something true. A few musicians, like the Beatles and Jimi Hendrix, eventually felt limited by their fans' demands and their record companies' hunger for hits. They had a difficult time trying to live up to people's expectations while still doing what was closest to their own hearts.

The late '60s and very early '70s was the right time for committed, impassioned, original music. Because of their huge numbers, the postwar baby boomers who came of age during this period affected society like no previous generation ever had. Many of these young people, well educated and outspoken, weren't content to allow their elders to dictate the shape and direction of the world. Across North America and the United

Kingdom, teenagers, university students, and working youth became more politically active. For a few years, they believed that they could bring about major social changes. They campaigned for the equality of women and racial minorities, and for peace at home and overseas. They supported politicians who favored new, progressive policies and they marched against those who didn't. There were protests and demonstrations. Many people were optimistic, not cynical; and the hippie ideals of love, peace, and equality briefly seemed within reach. Eventually, some of the ideas this young generation worked for would be accepted by mainstream culture.

Rock music was essential to this international community of young idealists. The photos throughout this book illustrate some of the issues that shaped and influenced the popular music of the day. Songs on the radio told listeners the news and helped shape their opinions. Musicians were forces for social change, either by writing and singing about it directly, or by exemplifying it in their performances and in how they lived. Stars didn't jump on political bandwagons just because it was trendy: Neil Young wrote "Ohio" because he was genuinely shocked by the Kent State shootings; CCR's John Fogerty composed "Fortunate Son" as his honest reaction to the hypocrisy of the American government's involvement in the Vietnam War.

Of course, just like any other era, the '60s produced a lot of forgettable music. There were goofy trends and manufactured clichés; for every one of the Beatles there were a hundred bands like the Monkees. But the best of the '60s music still sounds immediate and alive today. It still rocks. That's one reason "classic rock" is so popular, decades after the songs were written.

The muscians in this book, and many others, defined the shape of rock music long after their time in the spotlight. There isn't a songwriter alive who can

On August 28, 1963, a quarter of a million demonstrators marched peacefully across Washington, DC to the Lincoln Memorial in support of equal rights for African Americans. The "March on Washington" was one of the first events to be broadcast live on TV, nationally and internationally. For many watching, the speeches and performances eloquently expressed the goals of the civil rights movement for the first time: freedom for all.

honestly deny the influence of Bob Dylan's lyrics or Paul McCartney's melodies. Everyone who plays electric rock guitar has learned from Jimi Hendrix; all singers who bare their souls in performance have taken something from Janis Joplin or John Lennon.

The 10 chapters that follow took shape partly around this idea—how these musicians influenced everyone who came after them. Each chapter features a list of "musical descendants" who appeared in the decades following the '60s. In the work of these newer artists, we can hear the echoes of our 10 classic performers. Their influence will be felt, in one way or another, for a long time to come.

Also, these particular artists are profiled because of their popularity at the time, how much they defined and dominated a particular style of rock music, and how original and how potent they were when they were at the top.

A word about terms—such as "rock music." Rock is a category broad enough to include hard rock (for example, Led Zeppelin) and soft rock (some of the music by Crosby, Stills, Nash, and Young). It also encompasses, especially in its earlier years, music that might now be called country (Buddy Holly and early

In the mid-'50s, millions of teenagers around the world were hypnotized by Elvis Presley's revolutionary blend of swinging hips and rock and roll music. Elvis was a major influence on the following generation of musicians, including Bob Dylan, the Beatles, Jimi Hendrix, and Led Zeppelin.

Elvis Presley). There's folk-rock (some of Bob Dylan) and blues-rock (Janis Joplin) and jazz-rock (some of the Doors).

There's also the term "pop." Basically, it refers to the most successfully marketed, entertaining music of any given time. Although most pop music falls into one rock style or another, and most rock music is popular, the word "pop" suggests something lighter. Pop is intended as pure entertainment rather than as an expression of any serious ideas, whether personal or political. Some of our ten singers and bands have written the odd pop song—but, they were motivated by more than just popularity.

Another note, this one about time periods. The bands covered in this book are limited to those whose careers peaked during classic rock's heyday: from the mid-'60s to the early '70s. Before this period, rock music was still in its formative stages; after, it began to fracture into many genres and sub-genres. So, in this book, we're talking about 1964 until 1974. That's why you won't find Elvis Presley (too early), or AC/DC, or Bruce Springsteen, or U2 (all too late).

Still, there are many others who could have been included. Eric Clapton, Pink Floyd, David Bowie, Van Morrison, the Grateful Dead, the Velvet Underground, the Band, the Beach Boys, Joni Mitchell, Rod Stewart—here are another 10 who could make up a second book. Each has good reasons for being in this one. But whom would they replace?

Read the book, check out the music, and decide for yourself. Each chapter includes lists of the artist's best music. Pick up the albums if you can—they're the full show, a complete listening experience you won't get just hearing a song or two. Turn up the volume, flip through the pages, and rock on.

In Brief

Within 12 months—with two albums and a handful of performances—
Bob Dylan created a new style of music. Single-handedly, he exploded the old
ideas about what rock songs could say and sound like.

Dylan kicked off this amazing year by writing and recording one of rock's
most exciting, enduring songs. The following spring, he and his band played
a now-historic concert in Manchester, England. Because of what they
played and how the audience responded, this has become one of rock's most
infamous performances.

Bob Dylan
June 1965 to May 1966

Bob Dylan recording for
the album *Highway 61
Revisited* in June 1965.

The Band

Bob Dylan ★ acoustic and electric rhythm guitar, vocals, harmonica

The Hawks ★ Robbie Robertson ★ electric lead guitar
★ Rick Danko ★ bass guitar, backing vocals
★ Garth Hudson ★ organ, piano
★ Richard Manuel ★ piano, backing vocals
★ Levon Helm ★ drums, backing vocals

Dylan began as a solo performer but later added backing musicians. His mid-'60s albums *Highway 61 Revisited* and *Blonde on Blonde* feature many musicians, including some of the Hawks. The Hawks played most of his 1965–66 shows with him, using several different drummers.

The Background

BOB DYLAN, BORN ROBERT ZIMMERMAN, grew up in a small-town, middle-class family. His parents ran a hardware store in Hibbing, Minnesota. Like many young people in the '50s, Bob loved music. Idolizing Hank Williams, Little Richard, and Elvis Presley, Bob taught himself to sing and play basic piano and guitar. By high school, he was putting together rock and roll bands.

After graduating, he moved to Minneapolis and registered at university, but didn't last long. He spent more time learning songs than he did attending classes. Not long after, he took a gamble and headed for New York.

Arriving in the bitter cold of January 1961, with little money and no work, Dylan slept on floors and couches while trying to find places to play. He sought out and soon befriended the famous folksinger Woody Guthrie, who was slowly dying of Huntington's chorea, a rare disease. During Dylan's visits, Guthrie talked about his life, music, and politics. Dylan soaked it up. Some of his early original songs ("Song to Woody," "Talkin' John Birch Paranoid Blues") show Guthrie's influence.

Within six months, Dylan was attracting attention. Over the previous year, he'd abandoned rock and roll and re-invented himself as a folksinger,

Sometime around 1961, Robert Zimmerman changed his name to "Bob Dylan." It's often said that the name is a reference to the great Welsh poet Dylan Thomas, but Bob himself has never confirmed this.

accompanying himself on acoustic guitar and harmonica. Barely 20 years old, but full of confidence and energy, he had progressed enough by September 1961 to be playing at major folk clubs. He soon signed a contract with Columbia Records. His first album was recorded in just two afternoons and released in early 1962. Dylan was writing so fast ("I wrote five songs last night," he told a radio interviewer in 1962) that there were three more Dylan albums on the shelves by mid-1964.

By the early '60s Joan Baez was being called the queen of the folk-music world. She helped Bob Dylan early in his career by inviting him onstage during her performances. Baez earned a reputation as much for her political activism as for her music. During her 1962 tour of the Southern states, she shocked many by insisting that her shows not be segregated.

What's more impressive is that many of the songs written during these first years in New York are now classics. "Blowin' in the Wind" and "The Times They Are a-Changin'" sound as if they've been around forever. In the early '60s, these and other Dylan songs became anthems for young, politically active people, and were soon being sung all over the world. By 1964, Dylan had been branded as the voice of his generation. But he never wanted

FOLK MUSIC

Folk music is the traditional music of a culture, or music written in a traditional style. Many different forms exist around the world. It has its roots in songs played by ordinary people to entertain their friends and local communities.

Unlike rock, folk music often uses traditional melodies that are sung (often with the audience's help) and accompanied on acoustic instruments such as guitar and banjo. The words are often very important, telling old stories or carrying a social or political message.

In North America, folk music became more popular in the '30s, when Woody Guthrie sang about the hardships faced by displaced workers during the Great Depression. In his songs, Guthrie stood up for the poor while attacking rich businessmen and unjust government policies. His left-wing political message continued to be expressed in the '50s by musicians such as Pete Seeger; and by the '60s, folk songs had become rallying cries at demonstrations, on college campuses, and wherever people gathered to share ideas about making society equal for everybody.

Although folk songs don't get much radio airplay in North America, and folk musicians don't sell millions of albums, folk is popular at festivals across the continent and is still a force for change in many countries.

or liked that label, probably feeling that it carried too much pressure to conform to other people's expectations. That summer, he claimed, "I don't want to write for people anymore."

Throughout the rest of 1964, he performed across America and wrote material for his next album. His songs were on the charts, his concerts sold out, but he was becoming restless. Never predictable, never happy in one place for too long, Dylan moved away from acoustic music toward full-on rock. In early 1965, his album *Bringing It All Back Home* featured some of his new rock songs, which weren't as political as his previous folk tunes. Not all of his fans were pleased. Their reaction gave Bob a small taste of what was to come.

He went to England in the spring of 1965 with his girlfriend, folksinger Joan Baez. There, he performed with just an acoustic guitar—the last time he would do so for many years. By then, he was one of the most influential musicians around. The parties in his hotel room were attended by fans such as the Beatles and the Rolling Stones. But at the end of this tour, he briefly considered giving up music altogether. He was bored with his own songs.

Instead of quitting, on the plane back to the US, he began writing a song that would change him, his career, and rock music forever.

Over the years there has been much speculation about exactly whom the accusations in "Like a Rolling Stone" are directed at. But there are no definite answers. Some say that Dylan wrote it about Edie Sedgwick, a glamorous young New York actress and socialite he knew. Other people think he's targeting those who didn't believe in his music. But some fans are convinced Dylan is actually addressing himself in the song.

The Song That Changed Everything

"Like a Rolling Stone." It's just over six minutes long, from the first rifle crack on the snare drum to the wailing harmonica in the fade-out. Great sweeps on the organ fight for space with cascading piano fills and soaring lead guitar. In four long verses, Dylan, cool and mocking, spits strange, surreal images and accusations at an unknown, fallen target. She's a princess on a steeple, past her prime, now having to get used to living on the street with jugglers and clowns and Napoleon dressed in rags. The song's chorus is one of the most exhilarating ever written. You hear the chorus once and it stays with you forever.

Bob Dylan recorded the song in June 1965 at Columbia's New York studio. He brought in some of the hottest studio musicians around to join him. The song that would later come crashing out of radios and record players sounded raw and spontaneous because Bob and the band played it "live off the floor" (all together in the studio), and nailed it after only a few tries.

The song's impact was immediate. Unlike anything heard before, it was more insistent and majestic than other pop songs, and infinitely deeper. It was also twice as long. Back then, songwriters generally stuck to unwritten rules about length and format. Radio stations also preferred short songs,

Nuclear weapons have been tested on the Nevada Test Site, northwest of Las Vegas, since 1951. In the early days, observers had little more than protective glasses to shield them from the radiation. Though protests against nuclear testing were common throughout the '60s and '70s, there was a total of 925 tests conducted at the site between 1951 and 1992.

so they could program maximum advertising between tunes. Songs usually lasted three minutes or less. (Even now, singles rarely exceed four minutes.) But "Like a Rolling Stone" broke through this barrier, and the stations, swamped with requests, played all six minutes of it.

The song climbed the charts that summer. For many, "Like a Rolling Stone" redefined what pop music could do. Other musicians were inspired and sometimes intimidated. American rocker Bruce Springsteen later said that the opening shot on the snare drum "sounded like somebody had kicked open the door to your mind."

In 2004, *Rolling Stone* magazine ranked it the top song of all time. Even Dylan, who doesn't say much about his music, said, "'Like a Rolling Stone' changed it all."

With one song, Bob Dylan transformed himself from an earnest, politically conscious songwriter into something very different. No longer comfortable with his part in the protest movement, Dylan became someone whose substance and image many others would emulate years later. He was now cool and stylish, his eyes hidden behind shades, his ideas ambiguous, his answers ironic.

How Does It Feel?

"Like a Rolling Stone" was originally released in July 1965 as a single. On July 25, Dylan was booked to play at the Newport Folk Festival in Rhode Island. The yearly festival was one of the premier events celebrating the

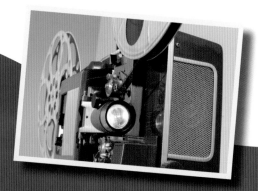

GREAT DYLAN FILMS

Dylan's work and life have attracted the attention of filmmakers throughout his long career. Their work has provided fans with rare glimpses of the elusive star. In 1967, *Dont Look Back* [sic] captured Dylan on his 1965 solo tour of England. It's a fascinating backstage look at Dylan at a turning point in his career.

A concert film, *The Last Waltz*, documents the Band's final show, performed in San Francisco in 1976. It features great guest performances by Eric Clapton, Van Morrison, Joni Mitchell, Neil Young, and of course, Dylan. The soundtrack album is super, too.

A retrospective documentary from 2005 called *No Direction Home* covers Dylan's career until the mid-'60s. The time period—and Dylan's role in it—comes to life with amazing footage of early concerts, plus candid interviews with Dylan and other musicians.

music and socialist politics of America's huge folk community. Dylan had first impressed the folk-music world as a newcomer at the festival in 1963 and was its star attraction in 1964. Organizers and fans expected great things from him once again.

But by the mid-'60s, folk music was starting to lose its hold on young people. Rock and roll was maturing, and songwriters like John Lennon of the Beatles, the Who's Pete Townshend, and Dylan were starting to express more complex ideas in their songs—which put rock in direct competition with folk. Folk purists considered rock music a "sell-out" motivated not by a sincere wish to change society for the better, but by the desire for money and fame. As a result, many Newport fans would have wanted to hear only acoustic instruments and earnest ballads, work songs, and left-wing politics coming from the festival stage.

Looking back, it seems strange that anyone was surprised by Dylan's Newport performance. He had, after all, just released an album of mostly rock songs featuring a full band. But the purists were shocked from the outset when Dylan appeared onstage dressed not in the protest singer's "uniform" of plaid work shirt and jeans, but all in black—with an electric guitar slung over his shoulder. And onstage with him was a full electric rock band.

As the band thundered into its first song, chaos erupted. The crowd booed loudly. Some festival organizers, along with older, traditional folk musicians, went backstage to demand the volume be turned down. Arguments broke out everywhere among the audience. Meanwhile, Dylan and the band played quickly through the song and into the next one—"Like a Rolling Stone."

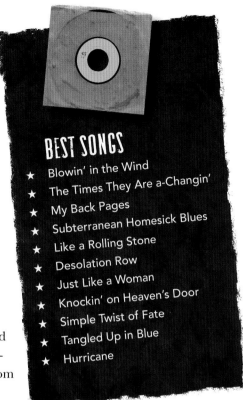

BEST SONGS

- ★ Blowin' in the Wind
- ★ The Times They Are a-Changin'
- ★ My Back Pages
- ★ Subterranean Homesick Blues
- ★ Like a Rolling Stone
- ★ Desolation Row
- ★ Just Like a Woman
- ★ Knockin' on Heaven's Door
- ★ Simple Twist of Fate
- ★ Tangled Up in Blue
- ★ Hurricane

Despite the song's popularity that summer, many in the Newport crowd didn't want to hear it. They kept booing throughout, continuing even when Dylan and the band finished one more song and left the stage. Some say Dylan was shaken by the reaction. Maybe he hadn't realized his performance might cause such controversy.

His three-song "electric" show at Newport 1965 was a turning point. After that, he and the folk/protest community parted company forever. The folk fans felt betrayed by their favorite son. And he—always ahead of his audience—had already moved on.

Highway 61 Revisited, the album containing "Like a Rolling Stone," was released a month later. Like its single, the album was revolutionary. Most of the nine songs had the same raw electric sound, and all featured lyrics that pushed the songwriting boundaries of the time. God and Abraham, graveyard women, hysterical brides and Jack the Ripper in the chamber of commerce—these images and more destroyed the idea that pop songs had to be simple and superficial, mere entertainment.

To Be On Your Own

Dylan's reception at the Newport Folk Festival may have prepared him for what was to happen during his upcoming tour, which ended up being just as controversial.

His touring band was a Canadian group known as the Hawks. Robbie Robertson, Rick Danko, Garth Hudson, Richard Manuel, and Levon Helm (the one American in the group) had worked for years around Toronto, backing rockabilly legend Ronnie Hawkins. Dylan offered them the chance to go on the road. Over time they became famous as Dylan's backup band. Later, when they recorded their own albums, they called themselves simply "the Band."

With the group, Dylan continued to create chaos with every performance. He would open with a solo set on acoustic guitar. This always pleased the crowd. But when the band took the stage for the electric half, pandemonium followed, mirroring Dylan's Newport Festival experience. Nevertheless, the Hawks' playing got louder, tighter, and more potent, achieving the tough, mean sound Dylan had been searching for.

During this period, Dylan's offstage life was also chaotic. He was constantly being interviewed. Some journalists didn't know much about new music, and Dylan grew tired of answering questions that sounded either antagonistic or ignorant. He began to give sarcastic or evasive responses, and so acquired a reputation for being uncooperative.

As the pressures of fame increased, he began using drugs more frequently. Instead of just wine and marijuana, Dylan was now popping amphetamines, which, in the short term, may have carried him through his frantic, high-energy schedule of recording sessions, rehearsals, concerts, and interviews. In the middle of all this chaos, he married Sara Lowndes, his new girlfriend. Early in 1966, their first child was born.

Over the winter, Dylan wrote new songs and recorded them whenever he and the band had a few days off. *Highway 61 Revisited* was still on the charts, but he wanted to create an equally impressive follow-up. As always, he worked fast. By spring 1966 the new album was almost ready. Called *Blonde on Blonde,* it would be released in mid-1966, less than a year after *Highway 61 Revisited.*

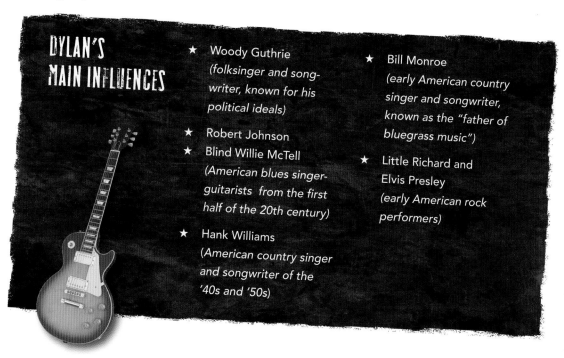

DYLAN'S MAIN INFLUENCES

★ Woody Guthrie
(folksinger and songwriter, known for his political ideals)

★ Robert Johnson
★ Blind Willie McTell
(American blues singer-guitarists from the first half of the 20th century)

★ Hank Williams
(American country singer and songwriter of the '40s and '50s)

★ Bill Monroe
(early American country singer and songwriter, known as the "father of bluegrass music")

★ Little Richard and Elvis Presley
(early American rock performers)

Though he was a champion in the boxing ring, Muhammad Ali refused to fight in Vietnam. The heavyweight boxer had an unusual mixture of brawn, wit, arrogance, and political conviction. In 1964, Ali won the world heavyweight title. He also joined the Black Muslims, an African-American religious and separatist movement. Because of religious and political beliefs, Ali refused the military draft and so was stripped of his boxing title and sentenced to prison. He appealed, and in 1970 won his case. He returned to the ring, going on to win the heavyweight title twice more.

Before then, Dylan and the band had to complete their world tour, traveling to Hawaii, Australia, and Europe. The trip concluded in the United Kingdom. There, the traditional folk movement was very strong, and as a result, press and long-time fans were especially negative about Dylan's new music. On May 17, the group played in Manchester. This show was recorded on tape and "bootlegged" (illegally copied, distributed, and sold). It later became mistakenly referred to as "the Royal Albert Hall" concert.

The performance was similar to Dylan's recent UK shows. During the second, electric half, the audience booed and shouted. In the silence before the final track is one of music's most notorious exchanges between performer and audience. Someone in the crowd—obviously feeling Dylan had "sold out"—shouts, "Judas!" in reference to the disciple who betrayed Jesus. The accusation echoes throughout the hall, sparking some cheering as the band gets ready for its last song. After a moment, Dylan steps to the mike: "I don't believe you," he says clearly. "You're a liar."

Then, off-mike (but still audible), he says to the other musicians: "Play it f***ing loud!" With that, the band launches into a scorching version of "Like a Rolling Stone," with Dylan stretching even further than on the studio recording, as if howling his defiance at the crowd. One moment, he and the band sound as if they're releasing all the frustration and bitterness they've built up over the last year's attacks. The next moment they sound as if they don't care anymore about what the audience thinks, instead just reveling in the joy of creating proud, powerful music. The drums pound, the bass rumbles, the guitars and keyboards screech

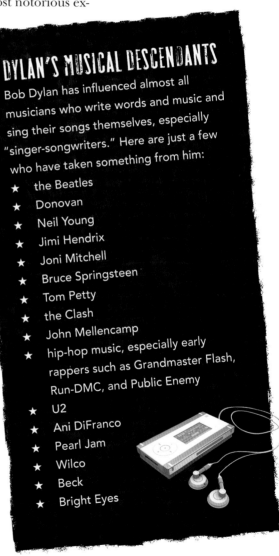

DYLAN'S MUSICAL DESCENDANTS

Bob Dylan has influenced almost all musicians who write words and music and sing their songs themselves, especially "singer-songwriters." Here are just a few who have taken something from him:

★ the Beatles
★ Donovan
★ Neil Young
★ Jimi Hendrix
★ Joni Mitchell
★ Bruce Springsteen
★ Tom Petty
★ the Clash
★ John Mellencamp
★ hip-hop music, especially early rappers such as Grandmaster Flash, Run-DMC, and Public Enemy
★ U2
★ Ani DiFranco
★ Pearl Jam
★ Wilco
★ Beck
★ Bright Eyes

and wail. Over top of it all, Dylan's voice is a challenge to people who had expected him to tailor his music to their tastes and then vilified him when instead he created something honest.

Since Then

A couple of months after his 1966 tour, Dylan crashed his motorcycle. After a brief hospital stay, he withdrew from the public to recover and rest, away from the pressures of his life. When he finally reappeared two years later, he looked and sounded very different.

From 1968 through 1974, his albums were heavily influenced by country music. Many people disliked this, wondering what had happened to him. In 1974, he resumed live performances, again with the Band. These concerts restored his reputation. After that, he released three more great albums with songs—some rock, some acoustic—that seemed inspired by the ups and downs of his marriage. In the late '70s, he became intensely religious and recorded three albums of spiritual songs. Several years later he returned to more mainstream rock.

Since the late '80s, Bob Dylan has been on what he calls the "never-ending tour." He changes band members frequently, traveling constantly, often returning to the same cities every year or two. At the same time, he continues to write and record. Now in his sixties, he's writing strong songs once again, with lyrics as rich and heavy as ever. He still snarls with the same edge he had at 25.

The critics have long been quiet. Now it would be difficult to find anyone who would admit to booing Dylan at one of those mid-'60s shows. He has become the most influential and enduring solo performer from the '60s, the inspiration for countless imitators, the subject of numerous books, movies, and tribute albums.

But those months between June 1965 and May 1966 still constitute a remarkably prolific, productive year, even in a career as long and amazing as Bob Dylan's.

In Brief

In the mid-'60s, the Beatles were on top of the music world. But at the height of their fame they stopped performing live.

Over the winter of 1966–1967, the Beatles holed up at Abbey Road Studios in London, England to create a record often ranked as the greatest rock album ever made: *Sgt. Pepper's Lonely Hearts Club Band.*

The Beatles
November 1966 to April 1967

The Fab Four: Ringo Starr, John Lennon, Paul McCartney, and George Harrison.

The Band

Here is the famous "Fab Four":

John Lennon	★	vocals, rhythm guitar, piano
Paul McCartney	★	vocals, bass guitar, keyboards, guitar
George Harrison	★	lead and rhythm guitar, sitar, vocals
Ringo Starr	★	drums, vocals

...plus their producer:

George Martin	★	production, arranging, occasional instruments

Lennon and McCartney wrote most of the songs, though George Harrison contributed as well. As their experiments in the recording studio progressed, the group used more unusual instruments and sound effects, with all four members contributing.

The Background

THE FOUR BEATLES were born into average working-class families during World War II in Liverpool, an industrial city in northern England. Life was hard in postwar Liverpool. Food and clothing were still rationed and most kids could only look forward to following in the footsteps of their parents. There wasn't a lot of fun to be had growing up—until the mid-'50s, when rock and roll arrived from America.

The young John Lennon got caught up in the excitement and learned a few chords on the guitar. At sixteen, he wasn't a great student, but was intelligent, rebellious, and a natural leader. It wasn't long before he'd recruited a few friends and formed his own group to play "skiffle," a British version of what we now call rockabilly. He called his band the Quarrymen.

Paul McCartney, two years younger, saw the Quarrymen play and was impressed with Lennon. After the show, the two were introduced, and McCartney played a few songs on the guitar. Lennon recognized that he had talent, and invited him to join the group. Later, McCartney's even younger schoolmate George Harrison was also asked to join.

Model fallout shelters held out hope that a family could live comfortably even in the event of a nuclear attack. From the late '40s until the early '90s, during an era called the "Cold War," Americans and Europeans feared that nuclear attack was imminent. Governments encouraged citizens to build their own backyard shelters. The Cold War was a result of political tension between the US and the Soviet Union, and their increasingly sophisticated nuclear weapons.

In 1958, Lennon's mother was killed, hit by a car driven by a drunken off-duty police officer. Lennon was devastated, but his loss brought him closer to McCartney, who had lost his own mother to cancer when he was just 14. Together, the two threw themselves into music, learning American rock and roll songs and practicing whenever they could.

Why "the Beatles"? American rock and roller Buddy Holly's backup band was called "the Crickets." McCartney and Lennon, both fans, named their own band after another insect. But they changed the spelling from "beetles" to "Beatles" perhaps to suggest the "beat" of their music and the counterculture of the "beatniks."

In 1960, the group, now calling itself the Beatles, got the first of several extended bookings in Hamburg, Germany. The long nights there developed the band's musical skills and showmanship. Lennon and McCartney also began to write their own music, partly to add songs to the sets. When Stu Sutcliffe, the original bass player, quit, McCartney took over playing bass. After a year and a half of going back and forth between England and Hamburg, the Beatles were a much better band.

In June 1962, they were given a chance to record at Abbey Road Studios. EMI Records owned the studio, which had traditionally been used by classical orchestras but was becoming well known for recording rock bands such as Cliff Richard and the Shadows. This session was the Beatles' first opportunity to capture the wild energy of their live performances on tape. It was also their first meeting with producer George Martin.

Martin was an established staff producer with EMI. At the session, Martin was more impressed with the personality, enthusiasm, and humor of Lennon, McCartney, and Harrison than with their music. He later admitted he was "quite certain that their songwriting ability had no saleable future!" But he decided to take a chance and offered them a recording contract, provided they replaced drummer Pete Best. The bandmates had already been planning to make this change—they'd met Ringo Starr while he was playing drums for another band in Hamburg. Now, they asked him to join, and the Beatles were complete.

The Beatles were booked for months at a time in Hamburg. It was a tough German port town where they had to play long sets at the club. There, the band learned how to put on a great rock show to entertain aggressive, demanding crowds.

Beatlemania

With George Martin's help, the group began recording. Lennon and McCartney had been writing furiously, working together on songs that would become their first hits, such as "Love Me Do" and "I Saw Her Standing There." Martin was forced to reconsider his opinion of their songwriting. In a unique way, they combined the sound of rock and roll, the energy of black music, and the strong melodies of earlier pop.

With the release of their first album, *Please Please Me*, in early 1963, the Beatles became very big, very fast. They had a distinctive sound and great original songs. In addition, they were young and good looking, with trendy clothes and long hair. They were given cute nicknames like the "Four Mop-tops" and the "Fab Four." They joked with the press, creating an adorable but mischievous image. The media loved them as much as the fans did. They were soon the most popular band in England. A Beatles craze swept the country: wherever they appeared, thousands of screaming fans and massive security followed. Every teenage girl had a favorite Beatle.

The mass hysteria of screaming crowds of mostly young, mostly female Beatles fans was nicknamed "Beatlemania." The British caught the bug during the summer of 1963 and it spread to the US when the band arrived in New York, February 1964. Teenagers would never be the same.

THE ED SULLIVAN SHOW

During the '50s and '60s, Ed Sullivan hosted the most popular entertainment program on TV. Broadcast live from New York every Sunday evening, his show was a variety show featuring comedians, dancers, acrobats, children's performers, and musicians.

Many famous rock musicians made their first TV appearances on *The Ed Sullivan Show*. Elvis Presley first hypnotized America on this show in 1956. Janis Joplin, the Doors, the Band, and Creedence Clearwater Revival all performed on the show in the late '60s.

But the most famous Sullivan broadcast came in 1964, when 73 million Americans—about 40 percent of the population—sat down on a Sunday night to watch the Beatles. That show set a record for the most viewers, and still ranks as one of the most-watched events in television history.

Born in 1901, Ed Sullivan was in his fifties when his show became popular. For a TV host, he looked unusually stiff and humorless on camera—obviously out of touch with the young rock stars on his stage. But he had a great ear for music, though he wasn't a performer himself. He wanted to be the first to showcase all the hot new bands, regardless of their style, appearance, or race. As a result, *The Ed Sullivan Show* enjoyed high ratings for two decades.

The Ed Sullivan Show finally ended in 1971, after 23 years. Sullivan had introduced over 10,000 performers to American TV audiences.

Fans of the '50s rocker Buddy Holly first saw him on TV when he played three songs on *The Ed Sullivan Show* in 1957. Holly was one of the first white rock stars to sing original tunes almost exclusively. His promising career was cut tragically short in 1959, when the plane he was in crashed, killing him and two other musicians.

The frenzy was called "Beatlemania." In early 1964, when the Beatles appeared on the popular TV program *The Ed Sullivan Show*, Beatlemania officially spread across the Atlantic Ocean. The band returned to tour the US in spring to find that their songs occupied the first five spots on the "Cashbox" singles chart. As they released more albums (*With the Beatles*, late 1963; *A Hard Day's Night*, mid-1964), scored more hit singles, and toured constantly through Europe, America, and Australia, they even eclipsed Elvis Presley in popularity—an achievement nobody had believed possible.

Their manager, Brian Epstein, made sure the band kept to a strict schedule of recording, record releases, and touring. He also made the arrangements to produce two movies, *A Hard Day's Night* and *Help!* Both films featured all four Beatles as central characters, deepening their connection with the fans.

The Beatles' lives became incredibly busy. In 1965, the band set a world attendance record at their concert in New York's Shea Stadium. That year they were also named Members of the British Empire by Queen Elizabeth. They kept up a brutal schedule of live performances, press conferences, and film work. Throughout all this activity, they found time to write and record.

"We had to grow up or we'd have been swamped," Lennon said, looking back. But as the Beatles got older, they outgrew their cute, cuddly image. Like many young people at that time, they began using marijuana regularly, and by the mid-'60s, were also experimenting with LSD. At the time, Harrison and Lennon in particular felt that drugs helped them to see

Bob Dylan, after hearing the Beatles on the radio, said, "They were doing things nobody was doing. Their chords were outrageous, just outrageous, and their harmonies made it all valid."

BEST ALBUMS
★ Please Please Me (1963)
★ Rubber Soul (1965)
★ Revolver (1966)
★ Sgt. Pepper's Lonely Hearts Club Band (1967)
★ The Beatles "The White Album" (1968)
★ Abbey Road (1969)

the world differently and to be more musically creative. Finally, led by Lennon, they became more political, speaking out against social conformity and the Vietnam War.

These changes in outlook were noticeable in the songs on *Help!*, *Rubber Soul*, and *Revolver*, their albums of 1965 and 1966. Together, these three albums feature songs that are as good as anything written in popular music before or since. The lyrics are poetic and insightful, and the music stretched the boundaries of rock. If the Beatles had recorded only these three albums, they would still be remembered as one of the top groups of the day. But all of this would soon be eclipsed by an album that defined the entire decade: *Sgt. Pepper's Lonely Hearts Club Band*.

A Day in the Life

In August 1966, the Beatles stopped performing live. Tired of the craziness of jetting around the world and singing to shrieking crowds, they decided to concentrate on writing and recording. Without the distractions of touring, their studio work blossomed.

The 1966–1967 recording sessions began with Lennon's "Strawberry Fields Forever." Lennon introduced the song to the group with just an acoustic guitar to accompany his voice. But at Abbey Road, the Beatles and George Martin added to this simple arrangement: McCartney played a mellotron synthesizer, producing the sound of flutes; cellos and brass gave the track an ominous air; and Harrison added otherworldly touches on an Indian harp. In addition, as an experiment they would repeat many times

Liverpool, an industrial port town in northern England, inspired a few of the Beatles' songs, including "Penny Lane" and "Strawberry Fields Forever." Today, tourists can visit a museum dedicated to the Beatles or take a tour of their old haunts.

after, they recorded layers of sounds on tape, and then played these backwards to add washes of noise.

The result was one of the most creative and surreal songs ever heard on pop radio. The Beatles released it in early 1967 as a double single along with McCartney's equally inventive "Penny Lane." Both songs were hugely popular and sharpened the public's appetite for the album to follow four months later.

Sgt. Pepper's Lonely Hearts Club Band disappointed no one. Even now, fans, musicians, and critics often rate this record as the high point not just of the Beatles' career, but of rock music in general. The thirteen songs display an amazing variety of styles and sounds, from hard rock (the title track) to psychedelia ("Lucy in the Sky with Diamonds"); ballads ("She's Leaving Home") to music-hall ("When I'm Sixty-Four"). The album was an ingenious concept, with the Beatles posing as an imaginary band performing the songs on the album.

Even the cover was creative. The photograph shows the Beatles gaudily dressed as the Sgt. Pepper band, surrounded by cut-and-paste images of famous people living and dead (Marlon Brando, Karl Marx, and Bob Dylan can be seen in the crowd). And something else was new: all the song lyrics were printed on the back of the album sleeve.

BEST SONGS

★ I Saw Her Standing There
★ Help!
★ Yesterday
★ Norwegian Wood
   (This Bird Has Flown)
★ Strawberry Fields Forever
★ Penny Lane
★ A Day in the Life
★ Hey Jude
★ Revolution
★ Something
★ Come Together
★ the *Abbey Road* medley
★ Let It Be

The Beatles were at their musical peak, and every song on *Sgt. Pepper* shows it. From the raw sound of the electric guitars in the title track to the circus surrealism of "Being for the Benefit of Mr. Kite"; from the hypnotics of "Within You, Without You" to the zany animal noises in "Good Morning Good Morning," the album ran over with so much creativity that fans are still dissecting and analyzing it, decades after its release. No album before or since made such an impression on the culture. The final track, "A Day in the Life," is the album's central song.

Lennon came up with the original idea for this song while looking through the newspaper. A rich man killed in a car accident, a patriotic war movie, civic officials counting holes in town streets—for him, these news stories offered little glimpses of what was impermanent, false, and trivial in life. He brought the unfinished song to Abbey Road in January 1967, and the band began working on it. Lennon played acoustic guitar and sang while the others added instruments. McCartney wasn't yet sure how his contribution, a section in the middle of the song, would fit in. They left an empty section on the tape during which an assistant counted to 24, marking off the time before McCartney's section would start.

The next day, the Beatles added parts to the basic track. Starr's echoey drums and McCartney's bass and vocals were recorded and blended into the mix. In the middle of the song, McCartney sandwiched in a completely separate song fragment: he jumps from Lennon's dreamy, ironic lines right into an everyday story about waking up late and rushing out of the house. Then Lennon's voice comes back in again, floating above the music, before returning to earth for the final verse.

Before the song was complete, the Beatles added two masterful touches. The first was to bring in a 41-piece orchestra to play through the empty section before McCartney's middle part. Martin arranged the orchestra's parts based on an idea of McCartney's. The musicians gathered one night at Abbey Road to play a monstrous crescendo, each instrument starting as low and quiet as it could and gradually climbing in pitch and volume until together, the orchestra reached an exhilarating climax. It worked so well that Martin re-used the part, just before the end of the song.

After the orchestra's final build-up, there is a brief pause—then the Beatles strike a giant E chord on three pianos, all their fingers hitting the keys at exactly the same time. The sound takes almost a minute to die out. This gradual fade is the last thing listeners hear on the album.

IN THE STUDIO

At Abbey Road, the Beatles did things in the recording studio that no one had ever done before. They and producer George Martin revolutionized the use of the four-track tape machine. By today's standards, with music being recorded on 24, 36, or 48 digitally separate tracks, then mixed together at the end, the four-track machine seems primitive. But Martin and the Beatles made the most of it, recording basic parts and then mixing these together to free up additional tracks. That they were able to create such intricate, complex songs with '60s technology is proof of how advanced they were as studio musicians, arrangers, and technicians.

1206 South Jackson
El Dorado, Arkansas
April 3, 1964

U. S. Labor Dept.
Washington D. C.

Gentlemen:
        I can only hope and pray
this letter will be read. I and
three other girls were so upset
we couldn't go to school today
because of an article in the
paper saying the Beatles can
not return to the U. S. until
the government gives their
approval. Maybe they didn't
follow the law of immigration
clearance order, but you
must all agree the teenagers
of the U. S. want them back.
Its none of my business but
they've just got to return
soon, please.

    I sincerly hope   you can
    ✗ ✗ can't spell.
        I'm very upset

give me some kind of reply to this letter. Please, if you can, answer if and when they will or won't return.

Very truly yours,
Janelle Blackwell

P.S.   This is no laughing matter to me or any other fan of the Beatles. Please reply ~~#~~ a letter back to me. This is a business letter and should be treated as such, Mr. Willard Wirtz, sir or whoever is reading this.
This letter ~~I know~~ know is not in good form of any kind. But I fell terrible.

I'm 15 and I fell like 80

The Beatles' late-1968 album is commonly known as "*The White Album*" because of its all-white cover, but its official title is simply *The Beatles*. It's a double-length album with 30 songs, many of which became classics. Although it is their bestselling album, *The White Album* features the four musicians working more as individuals than as a band.

Since Then

The Beatles reached a musical high point in 1967, though they were no longer actually writing together. More often Lennon and McCartney would add to each other's near-complete songs. Inevitably, the four were growing up and growing apart.

Just after the triumph of *Sgt. Pepper* came troubled times. Brian Epstein died of a drug overdose. Although the band no longer needed him to arrange tours, and had been critical of some of his recent business deals, Epstein had been in charge of their career since the early days in Hamburg. His death meant they were responsible for their own business affairs. Soon, they got into difficulty: they set up their own music company, Apple, but because of their lack of business skills, the company cost them a lot of money and caused bitter band disagreements.

In 1968, Lennon fell in love with a Japanese artist, Yoko Ono. He left his wife and son and began spending all his time with Ono. He even brought her to the recording studio. The other band members didn't like her constant presence or her comments on their music.

The band members were bickering more frequently. They argued about music, about who was in charge, and about their business affairs. McCartney became bossy while Lennon tried forcing the others to accept Ono as a virtual fifth member of the band. Harrison felt stifled creatively. Despite the strength of his songwriting, few of his compositions were included on albums. Starr actually quit in frustration for a couple of weeks in late 1968, but the others convinced him to come back.

Nineteen-sixty-nine was the last full year for the Beatles. It started with the impulsive five-song show they played on the roof of the Apple Records building one cold January afternoon. The band's performance was filmed and released much later as the conclusion to the movie *Let it Be*. An album of the same name was recorded early in 1969 but not released until May 1970.

Despite the spontaneity of the rooftop show, when McCartney tried to convince the others to work harder and return to live performances, no one else was interested. Lennon wanted more time with Ono and was also dealing with the effects of heroin addiction. Harrison and Starr were tired of being told what to do. Even Martin thought, "I don't want to be part of this anymore."

Their final recorded work was *Abbey Road*, issued in September 1969, ahead of the previously recorded *Let it Be*. What's amazing is that the Beatles were able to make great music despite all the animosity. *Abbey Road* is one of their best albums, with strong songs written by each band member.

The last piece on the album is an inspired, intricately crafted 16-minute medley of eight separate songs. McCartney, chiefly responsible for the medley, introduced new songwriting and arranging concepts from other genres, including theater musicals. Each song led seamlessly into the next, while music from one song reappeared two or three songs later, played on

THE BEATLES' MAIN INFLUENCES

★ Little Richard
★ Elvis Presley
★ Carl Perkins
★ Gene Vincent
★ Buddy Holly
★ Chuck Berry
   (early American rockers from the '50s and early '60s)

★ the Everly Brothers
   (American pop vocal duo from the '50s)

★ Cliff Richard and the Shadows
   (early British pop-rock band)

★ Motown
   (African-American rhythm-and-blues record label)

★ Bob Dylan

★ The Beach Boys
   (American rock and roll band noted for their vocal harmonies)

★ Ravi Shankar
   (Indian composer and sitar player)

★ Music-hall and ragtime songs from the early 20th century

The Beatles traveled to India in 1968 to study meditation and philosophy with an India guru, the Maharishi Mahesh Yogi. Lennon and McCartney returned to England after a short visit, but Harrison stayed much longer, and was permanently affected by India's peaceful spirituality and ideology.

different instruments. The last lines seemed to be the band's sad goodbye to each other and to the rest of the world. In the end, sang McCartney, the love we all take is equal to the love that we make.

With this, the Beatles' career was over. By the summer of 1970, the band had officially split up and the members were arguing with each other in the media. But it wasn't long before each Beatle released solo work. Harrison became involved with other musicians in raising money and awareness for disaster victims; his post-Beatles music grew more spiritual. Lennon moved with Ono to New York, where his songwriting became very personal and political. Soon, he had a huge hit with the famous ballad "Imagine." McCartney got married, had a family, and formed a very successful band, Wings, with his wife Linda. And Starr, always popular, recorded and toured with a variety of famous musicians.

In 1980, at the age of 40, Lennon was killed by a mentally disturbed gunman on the street in New York. And in 2001, Harrison died at 58 of throat cancer. Although two Beatles are gone, their best albums—including *Sgt. Pepper*—and their influence on popular culture will likely live on as the greatest of the last century.

In Brief

In late 1965, the Who released "My Generation," a song that immediately became the anthem not only for the "mod" crowd of London, but also captured the attitude of young people anytime and everywhere.

The Who's energetic stage shows, wild musicianship, and two later "rock operas" are their great contributions to classic rock. Their music and performance style heavily influenced punk rock of the '70s and hard rockers today.

The Who

November to December 1965

The Who—John Entwistle, Roger Daltrey, Keith Moon and Pete Townshend.

The Band

From 1964 until 1978, the Who's line-up was:

Pete Townshend ★ guitar, keyboards, backing and occasional lead vocals

Roger Daltrey ★ lead vocals, occasional harmonica

John Entwistle ★ bass guitar, backing and occasional lead vocals, French horn

Keith Moon ★ drums

Since 1978, when Moon passed away, the band has worked with replacement drummers and added other musicians while touring.

Townshend wrote nearly all of the Who's songs. Entwistle occasionally contributed songs, too.

A Typical Night

THE WEST END OF LONDON, England. It could be 10:30 p.m., late in November 1965. On a typical night, the rain drips off the eavestroughs up and down Goldhawk Road and pools deep in the gutters. But behind the big oak door of the Goldhawk Social Club it's jam-packed and hot, the air thick with smoke and sweat. By this hour on a regular Friday night, the crowd is impatient for the evening's headlining band—the reason everybody's here—to return for their second set.

On a night like this, nearly everybody squeezed together on the dance floor and sandwiched onto the couches at the edges is a "modernist," or "mod." They're young, clean-cut, and fashionably dressed. Their small, stylish Italian Lambretta and Vespa GS scooters line the street outside, below slick black-and-white posters advertising tonight's show.

The mods are ready to party. Many don't drink much beer, preferring instead to pop pills sold by dealers: "purple hearts," "French blues," or "leapers." These amphetamines are still legal here in 1965. When they're "pilled," mods talk fast, move fast, and dance like chickens with their heads cut off. And dancing is what a mod loves best.

The Goldhawk crowd doesn't have a lot of patience. Now, they're getting more and more antsy, waiting for the music to start again. The band is their voice and their spirit: unless the musicians appear soon, the crowd's unfocused energy will explode.

Tonight, they're here to see the ultimate mod band, the group adopted by the whole movement all over London.

The Who.

The mod "uniform" was high fashion with a twist. Girls, most with short hair, wore bright-colored dresses and skirts. Guys favored button-down dress shirts, Levis, and oversized parkas. Some wore well-cut European suit jackets and thin black ties.

The Background

Roger Daltrey, John Entwistle, and Pete Townshend all grew up not far from what would later become ground zero for the mods: Shepherd's Bush, in the working-class west side of London.

Townshend, who became the Who's songwriter, came from a musical family. His father was a professional saxophone player, his mother a performing singer. When Townshend was in his early teens, his grandmother gave him a guitar, and his father showed him some basic chords.

Townshend was bright, but painfully self-conscious of his large nose. "This (nose) seemed to be the biggest thing in my life," he said later. He also had a quick temper. Because of his shyness, he spent a lot of time at home, practicing guitar and then learning to play banjo. He joined a Dixieland jazz band, where he met schoolmate Entwistle, who played trumpet. Townshend didn't last long with the band, though, after getting into a fistfight with the drummer. Soon after, he switched back to guitar.

MODS VS. ROCKERS

Mods were recognizable to other mods, as well as to their archrivals, the rockers. The two groups battled wherever and whenever they crossed each other's paths.

For both groups, fashion and music were keys to membership in the gang. While mods looked sharp and clean-cut, rockers were leather-jacketed motorbikers who came from blue-collar families and looked a lot tougher than the mods. Rockers loved straightforward American rock and roll, whereas mods preferred an edgy mixture of rhythm and blues, soul, ska (a fast, early form of reggae) and homegrown rock.

Mods mostly lived at home with their middle-class London families and worked low-end office jobs. Then, to defy their conservative parents and bosses, they spent every penny on clothes and on going out. Rockers were factory men, mechanics, or construction workers who scorned their rivals' trendy outfits and behavior.

Mods would often go to clubs five or six nights a week, staying out almost until dawn—fueled by amphetamines—and then crawl in to work on a few hours' sleep.

As a trumpet player, Entwistle found it difficult to play the American rock and roll that he loved. "I really got very irritated when people could turn up their guitar amps and play louder than me," he said later. So he took up the electric bass, drawn to its low, menacing sound. He and Townshend then formed a rock and roll band.

Daltrey, who'd been a year ahead at the same school as Townshend and Entwistle, was already the leader of the best-known local band, the Detours. Daltrey was outgoing and direct, focused and driven. He had taught himself to play guitar, dropped out of school and formed the Detours. He met

Entwistle and invited him, and later Townshend, to join his band. The Detours played regularly in clubs around London. In 1962, Daltrey gave up the guitar to become the

John Entwistle made his own rudimentary electric bass guitar, on which he learned to play. Later, he constructed a better one.

group's front man and focus on singing. The band played or rehearsed almost every night and developed a local following.

Pub crowds loved the Detours not because they were great musicians—they weren't—or because they were great looking—only Daltrey had pop-star looks. Instead, the band was appealing to their (mostly male) fans because of their energy and attitude, their raw power and volume. There were a lot of better-known groups in England at the time: the Beatles were about to conquer the country from Liverpool, up north; and across the other side of London, the Rolling Stones were becoming a sensation. But the audiences in Shepherd's Bush felt a stronger connection to Townshend, Daltrey, Entwistle, and their band—local boys, just like them. The band

The audience goes wild at a Who concert. The Who became the third of the most popular and influential groups in British rock, along with the Beatles and the Rolling Stones.

Keith Moon started playing drums as a boy, but usually played too loud and powerfully for the bands he was in. His first love was American surf music, especially bands like the Beach Boys. By the time of his "audition" for the Detours, he was working for a plaster company, but within weeks of meeting Townshend and Entwistle, he was touring with the band.

members lived, worked, and drank nearby, and what they expressed through their music was what all the young people in their neighborhood felt. The passionate loyalty of local fans made it possible for the band to keep working, build their confidence and musical skills, and learn how to put on a powerful, dynamic show.

The Detours discovered another, more established band with the same name. Overnight, they became "the Who." Also, the band had been told that drummer Doug Sandom, who was ten years older, was the group's weak link.

Hearing that the Who were looking for a new drummer, 17-year-old Keith Moon showed up at a club one evening to audition, wearing a ginger-colored suit with hair dyed red to match. He downed a couple of beers for courage, then told the band that he was better than their fill-in drummer. Invited to prove himself, he jumped behind the drum kit, and during the next song, destroyed the bass drum, the drum pedal, and two other drum skins as well. "I figured that was it," he said later. "I was scared to death."

But he needn't have worried. The other three were knocked out by his energy, brash confidence, and aggressive drumming. They quickly asked him to join the group, and the Who was complete.

For a short time, they had a new manager, a new name—the High Numbers—and a new, mod look. But after releasing a single ("Zoot Suit" backed with "I'm the Face") in July 1964, the band attracted another management team that would help them break into the big time.

Kit Lambert and Chris Stamp invested some money in the band, and suggested the boys go back to their previous name, the Who, and focus

ENGLAND IN THE '60S

For teenagers in England in the '60s, life was much easier than it had been for their parents. A generation previously, bombs were falling on London, and food purchases were limited by the government because of wartime rationing. Even after World War II ended in 1945, the country took many years to rebuild its economy, industries, and health care system. The young people reaching adulthood in the '60s were the first generation to enjoy the benefits of these changes.

It was now possible to have fun, and music became a very important part of this. The English instantly took to American rhythm & blues and rock & roll as soon as they arrived from the US. Soon, British bands such as Cliff Richard and the Shadows were providing a domestic alternative to the American sounds. By the mid-'60s, British bands such as the Who, the Rolling Stones, and especially the Beatles were internationally famous. These bands were at the forefront of the "British invasion" that hit America as the middle of the decade approached.

Meanwhile, there were jobs and there was generally more money for everyone. England's old, traditional capital transformed itself into "swingin' London," one of the world's most fashionable cities. New immigrants arrived, bringing new energy. By the end of the decade, life in England was much more comfortable for ordinary people, and the country was known around the world as a rival of the US in fashion, culture, and music.

on writing their own songs. Townshend, who was already writing seriously, was especially excited about this proposition. The rest of the band was also enthusiastic.

Within months, their first single was released. "I Can't Explain" showed the Who at their best: Townshend's "power chords," Daltrey's gutsy vocals, heavy, rhythmic bass from Entwistle, and Moon's dynamic, unorthodox drumming holding everything together. Released early in 1965, the song was an immediate hit with the mods, who loved the energy, the beat, and the sentiment—*I feel good, but I can't explain why.* After their TV appearance on England's popular *Top of the Pops*, the single climbed to number eight on the charts and the band was nationally famous.

But in less than a year, the song "My Generation" would make them stars around the world.

By 1965, the Who were dressing in the mod style. Their signature "pop-art" outfits included Pete Townshend's famous Union Jack jacket. The British flag later became a key part of the Who's image.

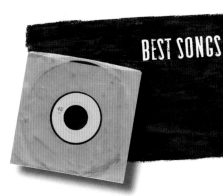

A Perfect Finale to a Great Night

There's movement on the stage and the lights flicker. The crowd on the dance floor at the Goldhawk Social Club presses forward as Moon sits down at his drum kit and fires off a shot on the snare drum. Then Townshend fills the room with a strummed D chord, the snare cracks twice more, and the band's into their summer hit, "The Kids Are Alright."

In less than a year, Townshend has become one of the best young songwriters to capture the energy of his generation in words and music. The Who's first album is due out soon, in early 1966. But tonight the band is saving the album's centerpiece, the song that will catapult them from local stardom to the world stage, for the end of the set.

As usual, the sound is deafening. The Who has the reputation of being the loudest band around, and it's obvious why. Townshend and Entwistle are each using two Marshall amps stacked atop one another, and the combined sound howls out of sixteen 12-inch speakers. Moon pounds his drums, and over top of it all Daltrey screams to be heard.

The band slides into a cover of the American rhythm and blues hit "Heatwave," and the dance floor is packed with jumping, gyrating bodies. Over the last year, the Who has learned from its audience how to harness and use maximum physical energy. Up on stage, the scene is almost as frantic as it is below. Townshend swings his outstretched arm like a windmill, attacking the guitar strings with the full force of his body. He leaps into the air at the same time, doing the splits. Daltrey takes the microphone off its

stand and tosses it high above his head, swinging it like a lasso and catching it just before singing his next line. Moon assaults his kit, a one-man demolition crew behind the drums. Only Entwistle stands still: his energy comes out in his active, forceful bass playing.

Another hit is next up: "Anyway, Anyhow, Anywhere," a popular original tune released in May 1965. But the best song is yet to come.

"My Generation" opens with thunderous power chords played in unison by Entwistle and Townshend. Then Daltrey enters in a unique way: he deliberately stutters his lines, like a tongue-tied mod "pilled" on amphetamines. Townshend and Entwistle answer each of Daltrey's lines with backing vocals of their own. The words are witty and scathing—the older generation puts down the young; the young have no respect for their elders. The first verse ends with lines that will soon become famous. The Goldhawk crowd has heard the song before and responds immediately, screaming the words back at the band. They may not really want to die before they grow old, but tonight they can believe it.

In the middle of "My Generation" comes a dazzling bass solo: Entwistle fires off four fast, fluid lines during the song's instrumental break. Daltrey's fingers snap and the drums tap to keep time. Then it's back into the singing again, the band raising the key and the intensity with every verse.

Sweat pours off the four musicians. The supercharged air inside the club feels like a sauna. The doorman opens the front door to let the room breathe, and the raging sound inside spills out into the still, wet street below. But on the dance floor, it's chaos. The mods jump on each other's backs, spinning, twisting, singing along. "My Generation" was written for this crowd, and the Who always play it as a final treat for their fans.

As the last chords ring out, Townshend holds his Rickenbacker guitar close to his amplifier, causing a high-pitched wail of feedback to howl out into the room. At the same time, Entwistle's hands snake up and down the neck of his bass, driving a mean, low rumble across the floor. Moon, pounding wildly on his tom-toms, kicks over his bass drum onto the stage next to Townshend, who responds by shoving the neck of his guitar into the roof tiles above the stage. Then, gripping the instrument around its neck like a club, he slams the guitar down hard on the wooden stage. As it shatters, the guitar, still plugged in, sends out ear-splitting shrieks over Entwistle's bass drone. Daltrey, meanwhile, slams the mike stand on the stage again and again as he screams out the song's final line, and Moon's drums collapse into a heap on the dance floor.

BEST ALBUMS

★ My Generation (1966)
★ Tommy (1969)
★ Live at Leeds (1970)
★ Who's Next (1971)
★ Quadrophenia (1973)
★ Who Are You (1978)
★ The Ultimate Collection (2002) [35-song greatest hits package]

The mods love it. "Auto-destruction," as Townshend calls it, has become a regular part of the Who's shows. It suits the rebellious, anarchic mood of their fans. The crowd responds in kind, unleashing its own form of destruction, until the bouncers step in. It's the perfect mod finale to a great night.

The screeching from Townshend's guitar finally dies out as he kicks over the amplifier stack, and the last sounds of "My Generation" are Entwistle carefully unplugging his bass and Daltrey wishing the crowd goodnight. Like the crowd spilling out of the club, the legend of the Who will not be contained.

Since Then

In the years after 1965, three things threatened to break up the Who. The first was the amount of equipment they destroyed. Despite brisk record sales and chart-topping singles, the band was in financial trouble. Each show might require hundreds or thousands of dollars to replace smashed instruments and demolished venues. Also, like other rock bands of that

When America's young president, John F. Kennedy, was assassinated in 1963, many young Americans felt as if they had been attacked and betrayed themselves. The nation grieved along with his widow, Jackie, and children, Caroline and John Jr.

time, the Who enjoyed wrecking hotel rooms. Moon got a reputation as a wild man by driving a limousine into a hotel swimming pool. Only toward the end of the '60s did the Who's earnings consistently cover their massive expenses.

The band's second problem was more personal. Townshend and Daltrey had notoriously short tempers and argued often, and sometimes came to blows. At one point, the other three got tired of Daltrey's intimidation tactics and kicked him out of the band. He returned, slightly mellowed. But the problems didn't end there. As Moon's alcohol and drug abuse increased, he grew unreliable. Entwistle was more stable, acting as referee. As the band members aged, they became used to each other and these problems subsided.

The Who proved to be one of the longest-lasting and most adaptable bands of the '60s. Mostly because of Townshend's vision and skill as a songwriter, the group grew far beyond its early association with the mods. By 1967, the mod movement was finished. The Who introduced themselves to the new growing audience of American hippies as a star act at 1967's Monterey Pop Festival. Two years later, they knocked out the Woodstock festival crowd with their power and passion.

Apart from wildly successful singles such as "My Generation," Townshend's revolutionary 1969 work *Tommy* ensured the Who's reputation as vital innovators in rock music. *Tommy* was the first "rock opera," a double-album story in songs. It provided a thoughtful, direct statement on celebrity, idol worship, and mass psychology as well as some memorable music. The album was a huge hit, immediately influencing other rock bands with its sophisticated blending of styles and recurring musical themes. Later, *Tommy* was made into a movie starring Daltrey and other famous musicians such as Eric Clapton, Elton John, and Tina Turner.

In the early '70s, the Who's success continued with strong live and studio albums. To many fans, 1970's *Live at Leeds* is the ultimate live album, full of raw energy and skilful musicianship. *Who's Next*, released the following year, reached number four on the charts and is ranked by *Rolling Stone* magazine as one of the best albums ever.

Another notable album from this time is *Quadrophenia*, another two-record story in songs. This time, the subject is the mods in London. The story is told through the eyes of Jimmy, a typical mod who lives the life experienced by Townshend and the others in the days when they played at the Goldhawk. Released in 1973, *Quadrophenia* inspired a movie that followed in 1979. Both the album and the movie triggered a mod revival in the early '80s.

The third crisis that almost broke up the band was more serious than smashed gear or band rivalries. In September 1978, Keith Moon died in his sleep from an overdose of sedatives.

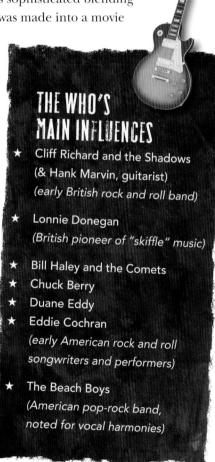

THE WHO'S MAIN INFLUENCES

★ Cliff Richard and the Shadows (& Hank Marvin, guitarist) (early British rock and roll band)

★ Lonnie Donegan (British pioneer of "skiffle" music)

★ Bill Haley and the Comets
★ Chuck Berry
★ Duane Eddy
★ Eddie Cochran (early American rock and roll songwriters and performers)

★ The Beach Boys (American pop-rock band, noted for vocal harmonies)

THE WHO'S MUSICAL DESCENDANTS

Of all the classic rock bands, the Who were the biggest influence on punk rock and power pop. Along with Led Zeppelin, they also shaped today's hard rock. Finally, Townshend's rock operas opened the doors for many "concept" albums since the '70s. Here are some bands influenced by the Who:

★ Pink Floyd
★ the Ramones
★ the Jam
★ the Sex Pistols
★ Generation X (& Billy Idol)
★ the Clash
★ the Replacements
★ Nirvana
★ Green Day
★ Pearl Jam
★ Foo Fighters

His wild, unstable life and excessive drinking and drug use had caused ongoing troubles and eventually led to his death. The rest of the band and the rock world in general were devastated. As the spark plug behind the Who, the most crazed and energetic member of a crazy, energy-driven band, Moon was irreplaceable. But Daltrey and Townshend were determined not to lose their band as well as their friend, so the following year, the Who launched the world tour they had been planning, now featuring their new drummer, Kenney Jones.

The final stage of their career still continues. Despite decreasing album sales since the early '80s, several "final tours" and Entwistle's death in 2002 of a heart attack, the band is still alive. The Who played at 2005's "Live 8" concerts. Meanwhile, Townshend has released several strong solo albums since the '70s and is still writing.

Most importantly, the energy, image, spirit, and music of the band and "My Generation" have influenced two generations of musicians since the Who's breakthrough in 1965. The destructive power and ideology of punk rock in the late '70s and the attitude and style of many contemporary bands are direct descendants of the Who.

Contrary to their most famous song's most famous line, Pete Townshend and Roger Daltrey may have gotten old, but their musical legacy has definitely not died.

In Brief

The Doors captured worldwide attention in the late '60s with a unique blend of jazz-rock music, theatrical concerts, and the dark, poetic lyrics and lifestyle of their charismatic lead singer, Jim Morrison.

A 1966 performance of their controversial song "The End" got the Doors fired from the club where they were playing. The show exemplified the drama and controversy that would later bring them international fame.

The Doors

August 1966

The Doors: Jim Morrison, Ray Manzarek, Robby Krieger, and John Densmore.

The Band

The Doors' lineup was the same from their formation in 1965 until Jim Morrison's death in 1971.

Jim Morrison	★	vocals
Ray Manzarek	★	organ, piano, occasional vocals
Robby Krieger	★	guitar
John Densmore	★	drums

The Doors are one of the few famous rock groups to perform live without a bass player. Ray Manzarek played all the bass parts in concert on the keyboard with his left hand.

The Doors generally wrote songs as a group, most often adding or expanding on Morrison's lyrics or melodies. Robby Krieger wrote a few of the band's biggest hits alone.

The Background

OF ALL THE MAJOR ROCK GROUPS of the '60s, the Doors are possibly the one most influenced by other arts, especially theatre and literature. Before forming the band, both Jim Morrison and Ray Manzarek were headed toward careers in film. In fact, if it hadn't been for a chance meeting in the summer of 1965, Morrison might have ended up a poet and Manzarek a movie director.

Morrison's father was an admiral in the US Navy, and by the time Morrison was in his mid-teens, the family had moved nine times around the US. By then, he was an insatiable reader, racing through books by the new, experimental American writers known as "the Beats." Excited by Jack Kerouac's novel *On the Road,* he devoured works by the other Beats. Then he moved on to the French writers of the 19th and early 20th century.

These books weren't light reading—many are notoriously dense and difficult to understand even for adults. But Morrison connected with them intuitively. He managed good grades throughout high school despite working only when he felt like it. He was a natural leader, although rebellious. School was not his biggest priority. He began filling notebooks with thoughts and observations, then started writing poetry.

Meanwhile, Ray Manzarek was growing up in Chicago, one of four brothers in a conventional, middle-class family. He and his brothers loved sports. But his parents also appreciated music, and this rubbed off on Ray. His mother used to sing, and she would often talk of her love for black blues music. Manzarek started piano lessons when he was seven, but it was only years later, when he mastered boogie-woogie style, that he really got enthused about playing.

He had many interests besides rock music. After high school, he completed a degree in economics while spending free time visiting museums and art exhibits. He formed a rock and roll band during his university days, but was also interested in modern jazz and symphony orchestra performances. Most of all, though, Manzarek enjoyed the cinema, so much so that he enrolled in the film program at the University of California, Los Angeles.

There he met Jim Morrison, who was also interested in writing and directing movies. Morrison loved literature, but saw film as the perfect combination of art forms. Manzarek and Morrison's mutual interest in film, combined with Morrison's aspirations as a poet and Manzarek's experience with different styles of music, later became a key element of the Doors' art.

One day in the middle of a baseball game, Ray Manzarek heard a blues song coming from a radio nearby. He dropped his bat and left the field to investigate. He later said that even though he never knew who the artist was, that radio song changed his life. It motivated him to search for blues on the radio, and later to seek out early rock.

After they both graduated in May 1965, Morrison announced his plans to move to New York. Manzarek tried to convince him to stay in LA, but the two parted. Later that summer, a chance meeting on Venice Beach sparked a collaboration that changed the course of their lives—and music history.

Though the Doors' theatrical tendencies were unique and compelling, they could be too much for club owners, the press, and even the police.

THE BEAT WRITERS

In the '50s, a group of American writers known as "the Beat Writers" or "the Beats" began to attract and influence young readers. The group included the novelist Jack Kerouac and the poets Allen Ginsberg, Gregory Corso, Kenneth Rexroth, and Lawrence Ferlinghetti.

Jack Kerouac's novel *On the Road* is a breathless, meandering story of a group of young drifters who drive aimlessly around America in search of adventure and meaning. Kerouac typed the entire first draft in three weeks, on one continuous roll of paper.

Kerouac, Ginsberg, and the others broke literary and social rules in their writing. Kerouac's famous novel *On the Road* tells the story of a group of young drifters who hitchhike back and forth across America, hanging out in black nightclubs, listening to jazz, smoking marijuana and drinking, all the time searching for meaning in their lives. Kerouac's sentences were long and rhythmic, overflowing with images and sounds—much like the freeform jazz he loved. After the Beats, adventure and freedom seemed possible in anyone's life—all that was needed was to jump a train or hitch a ride to the next town, and anything could happen. The Beats paved the way for other novelists, poets, and songwriters to make art out of their own experiences. Alienation, drug use, sexual experimentation, and social protest could all be discussed. Bob Dylan, the Grateful Dead, the Doors, Janis Joplin, and other musicians were influenced by Kerouac, Ginsberg, and their colleagues.

Kerouac, a true outlaw, drank himself to an early death; but many of the others lived to see themselves become cultural heroes to a whole generation.

Venice Beach, Summer 1965

One afternoon in July, Manzarek was sitting alone on the beach. He saw a figure walking through the water with the sun shining behind him. Manzarek thought the man looked like Alexander the Great, or maybe Michelangelo's *David*. Then the light shifted, and Ray saw that it was Jim Morrison.

Morrison approached, and Manzarek could see he was 30 pounds lighter than he'd been at graduation a couple of months earlier. He told Manzarek he hadn't gone to New York after all. Instead, he'd stayed in Venice, living on the roof of a friend's apartment building, experimenting with psychedelic drugs, and not eating. But writing—writing furiously. Not poetry this time, but songs.

Manzarek's mind started to tick. He asked Morrison to sing one of his songs. Embarrassed about his voice, Morrison refused. Finally, he relented and softly sang one called "Moonlight Drive."

The Beach Boys' songs of the early '60s glorified surfing as an essential part of the legendary easy-going California lifestyle.

Morrison and Manzarek called their band "the Doors." The name came from Jim's reading, specifically from a drug-influenced book by British writer Aldous Huxley called *The Doors of Perception* (the title itself was borrowed from a line by the 18th-century poet and mystic William Blake). The name summed up perfectly what the two wanted to do with their music: to be the doors between the known and the unknown, and to show people the way to explore the hidden corners of their own minds.

The melody was light and bluesy, the words alternately playful and mysterious. As Morrison sang, Manzarek was immediately swept away, hearing a whole band behind the voice: a jazz keyboard, a snaky slide guitar, and a punchy rhythm section bringing shades of light and dark to Morrison's strange, captivating lyrics—the best lyrics Manzarek had ever heard.

Encouraged, Morrison sang two more songs, both as bewitching as the first. *I know what I'm going to do with my life*, Manzarek realized in that moment. He knew that with his keyboard playing and Morrison's songs, they could get a band together and be successful.

Morrison agreed, but thought there was one problem: they had no singer. But Manzarek said that he, Morrison, had a great voice. They agreed Morrison would sing.

Next, the band needed a drummer and guitarist who were not only talented, but also approached music the same way as Manzarek and Morrison. Incredibly, Manzarek found them in his yoga class. Robby Krieger and John Densmore were both skilled players, jazz musicians who could also play hard rock and blues. The four began rehearsing and perfecting Morrison's songs, as well as their versions of older blues tunes. They soon got work at clubs around LA. From the beginning, the band stood out in many ways: their musical style, combining blues, jazz, and rock; their memorable original songs, built around Morrison's mystical, literary lyrics; and Morrison himself, instantly the talk of the town, a natural

FILM SCHOOL AND THE DOORS

In the mid-'60s, the film school at the University of California, Los Angeles was revolutionary. Famous European directors such as Jean Renoir and Josef von Sternberg ran the program. Some students went on to become famous in their own right—one graduate was Francis Ford Coppola, who directed the Godfather movies, among many others. Years later, the Doors tune "The End" was featured in Coppola's influential Vietnam movie, *Apocalypse Now*.

in the spotlight, commanding, cajoling, coaxing his audience to accompany him and the band on a musical trip into the unknown.

Live at the Whisky A Go-Go, August 1966

Out of the darkness onstage came the sound of a lone guitar as Robby Krieger played the delicate, vaguely sinister introduction to a new Doors song, "The End." The crowd at West Hollywood's Whisky A Go-Go—the heart of the west coast club scene in 1966—stopped talking, and a hush descended on the room. The music swelled, slightly Indian, slightly Arabic, as Jim Morrison stepped into the spotlight and began to sing.

Dressed in tight leather pants, his long hair flowing over his shoulders, he was a raw sex symbol who also appealed to the intellectual crowd, a rebel capable of inciting riots with his taunts, wild screams and physical contortions—but a rebel who could also quote literature and psychology.

Morrison wrote lines like nobody else—rich with surrealistic images and dark metaphors, invitations and temptations, sex and death, drugs and destruction. In addition, he had developed a stage persona that was part Elvis, part mystical shaman, and part wild animal.

The Doors' sensational residence as the Whisky's house band had lasted through the summer of 1966, and by August, they had developed many of the songs that would appear on their first album.

Now, quietly, Morrison sang of a parting and a journey. As the song picked up intensity, the words grew stranger. Behind him, John Densmore began to pound the drums as the piece reached its first crescendo before retreating again. Ray Manzarek's organ swirled lightly around the guitar then dropped to a whisper as Morrison gripped the mike and began to speak.

Almost in a dream state, Morrison spun a frightening, shocking tale, his take on the ancient Greek myth of Oedipus, the tragic hero who unknowingly kills his father and has sex with his mother. Morrison, swaying

MUSIC AND DRUGS

Artists of all types have always looked for ways to be more creative and reach for ideas outside the limits of most people's awareness. For hundreds of years, writers, painters, and musicians have used alcohol and drugs in an effort to get in touch with these deep inner worlds.

Drinking and drug use played a part in the lives of many 20th-century musicians. Early blues performers, often poor, drank cheap wine and spirits to lose their inhibitions while composing and playing. Some of the best-known jazz players—like Charlie Parker, Billie Holiday, and Bill Evans—were regular users of hard drugs. When Evans, a long-term heroin addict, passed away, his death was called "the longest suicide on record."

In the '60s, many young people experimented with marijuana, psychedelic drugs such as LSD, and even heroin. Many rock musicians, sometimes introverted and insecure, felt that drugs could help them conquer the nervousness of being onstage in front of huge crowds. But rock, too, has had its share of drug casualties. For every musician able to overcome the physical and mental effects of serious drugs (like Keith Richards, John Lennon, and Jimmy Page), there has been another whose self-destructive habits led to a tragically early death.

Ultimately, the survivors seem to agree that they could have found the same creative boost without the drugs.

The famous variety show host Ed Sullivan is remembered for the restrictions he placed on his guest performers. When the Doors were scheduled to appear in 1967, Sullivan made Morrison promise not to sing the line "we couldn't get much higher" when they performed "Light My Fire." Sullivan's attitude reflected the anti-drug position of mainstream America. But when the cameras were rolling, Morrison not only sang the words but clearly articulated them. Sullivan, furious, banned the Doors from the show thereafter.

on the mike stand, eyes half shut, spoke slowly, and the mesmerized Whisky audience hung on each word. This was very different from any other rock band they'd ever seen.

As Morrison's killer moved through the dark toward his climactic act, the music rose again, this time to a deafening peak, with drums, guitar, and organ hammering together as a kind of Greek chorus behind Morrison's drawn-out, anguished screams. The stage lights flashed as Morrison sank to the ground, his movements echoing the story, the instruments now humming softly again. He rose slowly to sing his last few lines. The lights dropped again, and, eleven minutes after it had begun, "The End" was finished.

The crowd erupted, shrieks and whistles mingling with boos and cheers. While many listeners loved the song, others were scandalized by the overt references to violence and incest. Though the Doors were attracting growing crowds to their Whisky gigs, this particular show was too much for the club's manager. He came backstage after the set and immediately fired the Doors and kept them off the club's stage until the furor over their performance died down.

BEST SONGS

- ★ Break on Through
- ★ Light My Fire
- ★ The End
- ★ People Are Strange
- ★ Hello, I Love You
- ★ Roadhouse Blues
- ★ L.A. Woman
- ★ The WASP
- ★ Riders on the Storm

BEST ALBUMS

★ *The Doors* (1967)

★ *Strange Days* (1967)

★ *Morrison Hotel* (1970)

★ *L.A. Woman* (1971)

It didn't matter. The following year, 1967, was probably the best of the Doors' career. They released their first album, called simply *The Doors*. It still stands as one of the best debut albums in rock history, a confident and distinctive record with songs that became classics (including those songs Morrison had sung for Manzarek on Venice Beach). It also featured the band's biggest hit, "Light My Fire." This last song was a number-one song through the summer. Near the end of the year they released their second album, the equally successful *Strange Days*.

But like a classical myth, the Doors' climb to the top would be followed soon after by a sudden fall from grace. Like Greek heroes, their greatest strength—the risk and theatrical drama in their music and their lives—would be the very thing that brought them down.

Since Then

The good times continued for the Doors through 1968. They released another successful album and expanded further into film by creating a short movie for their song "The Unknown Soldier." This was a groundbreaking piece created by Morrison and Manzarek, an early music video inspired by the young men drafted into military service to fight the Vietnam War. The film, shown during concerts, featured Morrison being crucified. Although again controversial, the song and film increased the band's status among young people who were opposed to the escalating war. The Doors' dark themes seemed to reflect the sinister events of the late '60s, days in which Martin Luther King and Robert Kennedy, two of America's brightest and most hopeful leaders, were brutally assassinated.

However, there now appeared signs of the problems that would cause so much future trouble for the band: namely, Morrison's drinking, drug abuse, and increasingly erratic behavior. He himself admitted that he wasn't interested in the middle ground, opting instead for life's extremes.

Morrison had always been fascinated by the mythic lives of writers who lived on the edge in order to heighten their perception of the world and their own creativity. Now, as one of the world's biggest rock stars, he was able to indulge in every excess. He became an alcoholic, capable of consuming huge quantities of beer, wine, and hard liquor without passing out. He used different drugs, mostly marijuana and LSD, and he may have experimented with peyote and heroin.

But Morrison's desire to push boundaries could affect his judgment onstage. He was arrested several times for what he said and did in concerts. The most serious incident was in Miami in 1969, where he was charged with indecent exposure. The media and the public began to focus more and more attention on these episodes, instead of on the Doors' music.

Morrison became frustrated by his fame as a rock star, when really he wanted to be a serious writer.

The Doors made a movie of their antiwar song, "The Unknown Soldier," in 1968. In performance, guitarist Robby Krieger would point his guitar at singer Jim Morrison, while drummer John Densmore mimicked the sounds of firing guns. Morrison would fall down on stage as if shot.

The other three Doors disbanded the group a couple of years after Morrison's death. But since then, re-issues of Doors albums, movies about the band, and a flurry of books about Morrison's life and work have turned another generation of fans on to their unique sound and style of music.

JIM MORRISON'S GRAVE

Jim Morrison lies buried in the heart of perhaps the world's most famous graveyard. The Père-Lachaise Cemetery, in Paris's historic eastern district, is the final resting place of some of the most celebrated musicians, painters, writers, philosophers, and statesmen from France and other countries. It's a brooding, baroque place, with beautiful, sculpted tombs packed between rows of ancient trees.

Morrison was laid to rest in July 1971, and since that time, his grave has been a very popular pilgrimage for Doors fans from around the world. Fans who visit the grave leave flowers, notes, and photos—and paint graffiti on surrounding tombs. The cemetery management has posted a full-time guard to make sure visitors show proper respect for other graves close by.

Buried among the world's great artists, Morrison finally found in death the company he'd searched for during his life.

Although his books of poetry were published, it wasn't enough for him. He almost quit the band to concentrate on writing. Manzarek and the others convinced him to stay, for despite his increasing unreliability, they recognized his rare talents and valued his warmth, humor, and intelligence.

Morrison stayed with the band until the end of 1970. He continued to drink heavily, putting on weight and growing a beard, maybe trying to escape his image as a sex symbol. He also had short, turbulent affairs with famous women, including Janis Joplin and Nico, a singer in the band the Velvet Underground. His sexual behavior, like his substance abuse, was a favorite theme for the media, and distracted him and the Doors from their music.

THE DOORS' MAIN INFLUENCES

★ Federico Fellini
★ Jean-Luc Godard
★ Sergei Eisenstein
   (art-house movie directors)

★ Muddy Waters
★ Howlin' Wolf
★ John Lee Hooker
★ Little Richard
   (blues and early rock pioneers)

★ Bill Evans
★ John Coltrane
★ McCoy Tyner
   (jazz musicians and composers)

★ JS Bach
★ Claude Debussy
   (classical composers)

Finally, Morrison could not continue fronting the Doors. He was unhealthy and had lost his enthusiasm for the role. The band decided to take a break, and early in 1971, Morrison and his girlfriend, Pamela Courson, moved to Paris so he could rest and write.

Sadly, the recovery never happened. In July, one month after the release of *L.A. Woman*, the Doors' final album, Morrison died in the apartment he shared with Courson. Only 27, he had apparently suffered a heart attack while in the bathtub. By the time the Doors' manager arrived in Paris, the death certificate had been signed and the coffin was sealed. Morrison was buried the following day in Paris's ancient Père-Lachaise Cemetery with only five people present.

Courson was alone when she discovered Morrison's body, and the doctor who signed the death certificate could not be found later. Because

In 1970 the band released the album *Morrison Hotel*, with the classic drinking song "Roadhouse Blues." Their live album that year featured the very long poem, "Celebration of the Lizard," performed by Morrison over minimal music. This poem is what gave Morrison his nickname "the Lizard King."

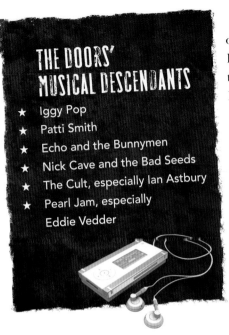

THE DOORS' MUSICAL DESCENDANTS

★ Iggy Pop
★ Patti Smith
★ Echo and the Bunnymen
★ Nick Cave and the Bad Seeds
★ The Cult, especially Ian Astbury
★ Pearl Jam, especially Eddie Vedder

of these strange circumstances, and as Morrison had sometimes talked about staging his own death to escape his fame, rumors that he was alive and living somewhere else under another name began to circulate. Regardless, Morrison's grave became the main attraction at the famous cemetery. Even in death, Morrison couldn't leave behind his reputation as the most controversial, cerebral, and provocative rock star of the late '60s.

In Brief

A relative newcomer to rock music stepped onto the stage at the 1967 Monterey Pop Festival and caught the world's attention. In that single performance, Janis Joplin, with Big Brother and the Holding Company backing her, became the most famous female vocalist of the decade. This young woman from a small, conservative Texas town redefined how white female singers could look, act, and sound.

Joplin's career was short but spectacular. She burned as brightly as any '60s star, never more than on the night of her inspired performance at Monterey.

Janis Joplin
June 1967

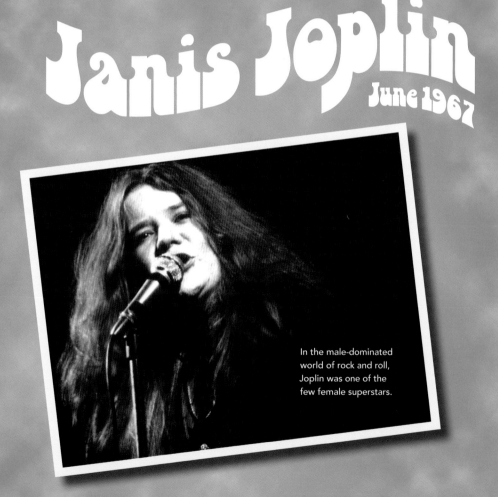

In the male-dominated world of rock and roll, Joplin was one of the few female superstars.

The Band

Joplin's back-up band at the Monterey Pop Festival was Big Brother and the Holding Company. The group included:

James Gurley ★ guitar
Sam Andrew ★ guitar
Peter Albin ★ bass guitar
Dave Getz ★ drums

Joplin co-wrote some of her songs with others. But she was most famous because of her singing, as she performed powerful interpretations of other people's songs.

Backstage at Monterey

IT WAS A WARM AFTERNOON in the middle of June 1967, the beginning of what would later be called "the summer of love." Janis Joplin stood backstage at the Monterey Pop Festival, waiting to perform with her band, Big Brother and the Holding Company. Joplin and the band had a local following in San Francisco, but the 200,000 fans at Monterey that weekend were being entertained by some of the biggest names in music, including the Who and Jimi Hendrix, as well as west-coast favorites Jefferson Airplane and the Grateful Dead.

Joplin was nervous. Just 24, she had been Big Brother's lead singer for only a year. Prior to that, she'd drifted around, singing occasionally in folk clubs in Texas and Louisiana. A mere two years before Monterey, she was living with her parents in her hometown—Port Arthur, Texas—taking classes at the local secretarial school.

Now, she was about to sing at America's first major rock festival. There were more than 30 acts on the bill, and 300 reporters from major papers and magazines as far away as London, England. Representatives from international record companies were there to scout the bands. A strong performance would make her an instant star; a weak performance, and she might be forgotten.

Outside the performing area, marijuana smoke wafted through the afternoon air. Artists had set up booths selling clothes, jewelry, flowers, and anti-Vietnam War posters. Rock stars Joplin had only read about—like Brian Jones of the Rolling Stones—hung around the stage watching the show. A film crew was set up, capturing the performances for a movie about the festival. And everywhere, there were people, more people than the entire population of Joplin's hometown.

At Monterey, Joplin and her band faced the biggest test in their young careers. She waited in the wings for the band on stage to finish playing and for the announcer to introduce her group. Whatever she did as soon as she stepped out on the stage would make or break her.

The sleepy coastal town of Monterey was a retreat for harried city folk. But in June 1967, the crowds arrived with the Monterey Pop Festival. The event was remarkably peaceful —even the local police were happy. Unlike Woodstock two years later, all proceeds from the Monterey Festival went towards charity. The musicians performed for nothing more than room and board, though some left with a record contract.

BESSIE, BIG MAMA, AND THE BLUES

Two of Janis Joplin's biggest influences were African-American blues singers. The "blues" is an African-American folk music style, born out of years of slavery and oppression. Its distinctive feature is its melancholy sound. As African Americans moved from the rural Southern states to the cities in the '40s, the blues found a wider audience, and later gave rise to rhythm and blues (a danceable version) and rock and roll.

Both Bessie Smith and Big Mama Thornton were hugely talented, determined women who found success despite the challenges of poverty and discrimination.

Smith's short life began in 1894 in Tennessee. By the time she was nine, she'd lost both her parents. She grew up earning money for food by singing and dancing on the streets. At 18, she left home to perform with a traveling theater company and began to develop her own powerful singing style.

In the early '20s, Smith began to record blues songs, which made her very popular and well paid, although black musicians in those days made far less than their white peers. She played with the great jazz trumpeter Louis Armstrong, touring and making blues and swing records. But in 1937, she was killed in a car accident.

Willie Mae ("Big Mama") Thornton, born in 1926, had a similar childhood to Smith's. At 14, she ran away to join a traveling show as a singer.

In 1953, Thornton (nicknamed "Big Mama" because of her six-foot, 350-pound frame) recorded her biggest-selling record. Called "Hound Dog," it was an up-tempo blues song that Elvis Presley re-recorded a few years later. Although Thornton claimed to have written the song, she was never given credit and received no payment when Elvis's version sold five million copies.

Her career finally got a break when Joplin recorded her song "Ball and Chain." This restored Thornton's popularity after a low period. Despite poor health, she continued recording and touring successfully until her death in 1984.

Both Smith and Thornton developed the blues as a style and made it more popular among both black and white audiences. They also blazed a trail that future female singers—like Janis Joplin—could follow.

The Background

It was a very long journey from the stifling confines of a small Southern town to the stage at Monterey. Janis Joplin was born in 1943 in Port Arthur, in east Texas near the Louisiana border. Like many people in Port Arthur, her father Seth was a Texaco oil company employee. Her mother, Dorothy, worked at the Sears department store before having Janis and her younger siblings, Laura and Michael.

The average small town in Texas was far too quiet for Joplin's restless and adventurous spirit.

Though conservative and strict, Joplin's parents were loving. Her mother taught her some piano, and her father played her his favorite blues records—not popular music among white Texans. Books, ideas, and educated opinions were encouraged in the Joplin house. Her parents taught her to be polite, but also to think for herself.

The independence that her parents encouraged soon got her into trouble, though. She was talented in art and a good student, but she talked too much for some teachers' liking. Girls were supposed to be quiet and obedient—Janis asked too many questions and was too lively. She just couldn't conform, at a time when standing out was strongly discouraged.

By the ninth grade, there were two very different sides to Joplin. On one hand, she was the girl who sang at the Christmas pageant, drew posters for the local library, and joined a reading circle. On the other, she

During high school, Joplin became friendly with a small group of boys, who, like her, longed for something more in life. Together, they read the new, experimental "Beat" writers and drove across the Sabine River into Louisiana in search of adventure. These friends were pivotal in broadening her horizons.

AMERICA IN THE '50S

The '50s were very conservative years in America. Most adults had lived through the Great Depression and World War II, and their priority now was to work hard, make money, and do what the boss, the company, and the government said. Not many people wanted the boat rocked with new ideas or defiant behavior. In Southern rural towns, religion and racial segregation helped to maintain old-fashioned ways of life.

Elsewhere in America, though, society was beginning to change. Big cities such as New York, Chicago, and San Francisco were much less conformist than the small towns. New fashions and ideas gradually emerged. By the late '50s, early rock and roll was making its first impression on young people, providing them with a musical alternative to the big bands and "crooners" of their parents' generation.

Urban white teenagers and university students were also starting to explore African-American culture. To them, jazz musicians such as Charlie Parker and John Coltrane seemed impossibly cool, dangerous, and sophisticated. Institutionalized racism began to crumble, sparked by the courage of activist Rosa Parks, civil rights leader Martin Luther King, and their supporters, both black and white.

was the girl who swore, told dirty jokes, and drank with the less reputable crowd. Like many young people who build up a tough exterior, Joplin was compensating for the insecurity she felt inside.

As a little girl, she had been cute. But as she became a teenager, her looks changed: her curly hair got frizzy, she put on weight, and developed serious acne. High-school girls in small-town Texas in the '50s were expected to compete for positions as cheerleaders or "Most Popular Girl." Joplin, with her independent mind, her bad language, and now her looks, which wouldn't have been considered conventionally attractive, didn't have a chance. So she rebelled.

When she was criticized for her behavior, she became even more defiant, clashing with her teachers and her mother. She discovered that although she wasn't the prettiest girl at school, she could attract attention from boys by showing she was willing to experiment with sex.

Most of Joplin's classmates were conservative. The boys planned to finish high school and get local jobs with the oil company. Some might go on to study business or engineering at an east-Texas university. Most girls hoped to marry young, prepared to give up whatever career interests they might have had in order to be good wives and mothers. To someone like Joplin, trapped in a place that didn't understand her or tolerate her differences, the world beyond her town must have looked irresistible.

BEST ALBUMS

★ *Cheap Thrills* (1968) [with Big Brother and the Holding Company]

★ *Pearl* (1971) [with the Full Tilt Boogie Band]

★ *Janis Joplin's Greatest Hits*

In the late '60s, San Francisco's Haight-Ashbury district attracted thousands of young Americans who wanted a "revolution," a complete overthrow of accepted values, politics, and personal style. The once working-class area transformed into "Hippie-Land," practically a foreign country for conservatives. Passes, such as the one pictured here, were given to conservative "foreigners" who visited the area.

The way Joplin looked often raised eyebrows. She wore pants more often than the typically feminine skirt or dress; much of her wild, multi-colored wardrobe was made by a friend. She let her curly hair hang loose, adorning it with scarves and streaks of bright color. Rings, bracelets, and necklaces jangled all over her body. Finally, the fact that she didn't wear make-up was considered a radical statement for a female celebrity. Her strident, liberated style often drew criticism.

Joplin found a small group of likeminded people. Together they began to visit nightclubs to listen to live blues bands. This music—the songs of the lonely, the oppressed, those suffering pain and loss—touched her in a way that the tame, bubbly tunes on pop radio could not. She began her love affair with the blues and the great black female singers who interpreted those songs.

Lonely and unsure about her future, Joplin made a choice. What she saw and heard beyond the narrow limits of her hometown convinced Joplin that she had to get out of Port Arthur.

Full Circle

Ten years later, Big Brother and the Holding Company hit the stage at Monterey. Joplin came out hard, as always, with one of her own songs, "Down on Me." No longer nervous, she stalked the stage, her voice rising from a whisper to a scream and cascading sweetly back down again as she seduced and stunned the huge crowd. From the opening, it was obvious that this would be a great set. Behind her, Big Brother picked up the intensity of the performance, and together they drove through three more dynamic songs before the final number, the show-stopping "Ball and Chain."

By this time in her career, Joplin had developed a big, powerful voice and a commanding stage presence, like her blues idols. In earlier performances, San Francisco crowds had been knocked out by her highly charged singing. Female singers at that time were either sensitive folk performers like Joan Baez or sophisticated jazzers like Ella Fitzgerald. Nobody imagined a white woman with the vocal style and raw energy of a black blues singer could front a rock band. Unlike her female contemporaries, Joplin also took some cues from male rock stars. She sang with energetic abandon, wore outrageous outfits and pranced around the stage like it was her own living room.

She had also developed a reputation as a party girl. By 1967, she was a heavy drinker, a regular marijuana smoker, and a frequent user of hard drugs like "speed" (amphetamines) and heroin. The media repeated stories of her wild behavior. Joplin played along with her public image— but those close to her knew her other shy, sweet side.

When Joplin sang "Ball and Chain" at the Monterey Festival, she made the song hers, pouring her unhappiness into the verses. After four and a half riveting minutes, the band stopped playing altogether, leaving Joplin alone at the front of the stage. She continued, improvising words and melodies, creating the story as she went, until at last she wasn't singing at all, just talking to the crowd. She told them that she didn't understand the sadness in the world, that if they only had one day to show love for someone, then they should take the chance to do it, because the chance wouldn't come again.

BEST SONGS

* Piece of My Heart
* Cry Baby
* Me and Bobby McGee
* Mercedes Benz
* Down on Me
* Ball and Chain (live, Monterey Pop soundtrack, released 1997)

WOMEN'S LIBERATION

Politics, race relations, and the relationship between generations all changed during the '60s—and so did women's role in society.

A decade earlier the civil rights movement had begun; its goal was to balance the inequalities between blacks and whites. Similarly, the movement known as feminism, or "women's lib," aimed to increase the status of women. Feminists supported the right of women to choose their own careers and be paid equally for their work. They also believed that men should share the domestic workload.

Before the '60s, earlier feminists, known as suffragists, campaigned for women's right to vote. Thanks to the groundwork laid by these pioneering activists, women of the '60s were more confident in their demands. By this time, more women were going to university. With greater education, young women didn't feel as much pressure to give up their own careers for marriage. The legalization of the birth control pill gave women power over reproduction and helped them avoid unwanted pregnancies. This new freedom was responsible for the so-called "sexual revolution" of the '60s. Finally, strong women began to raise their voices. Singers such as Aretha Franklin, Janis Joplin, and Jefferson Airplane's Grace Slick lived larger than life, giving other women role models to follow.

By the mid-'70s, the main ideals of the movement were becoming a more accepted part of mainstream culture.

In the '70s, a popular cigarette advertisement tried to appeal to women by linking freedom with smoking cigarettes, telling women that they'd "come a long way." Many disagreed. The Equal Rights Amendment, which would make equality between men and women part of the US Constitution, was passed by Congress in 1972, but it has still not been ratified by every state.

Despite her superstar status, Joplin was a kind and thoughtful friend. She sometimes cooked meals and baked for others, and her frequent letters home showed a loving, attentive daughter and sister who needed her family's affection, despite her fame. She told them excitedly about her music, homes and cars, pets, and about each new hopeful relationship.

The crowd hushed, sensing the honesty in front of them, seeing someone whose music came from the very center of who she was. Then Joplin softened the spell with a joke, and sang again, bluesy ad-libbed lines, her voice dancing around the melody like a guitar or a sax, rising impossibly high, then stuttering down low before swooping back up again to finish, after almost four minutes of improvising, on the song's last words—"like a ball and chain."

Their show was such a hit that Janis Joplin and Big Brother and the Holding Company were asked to repeat "Ball and Chain" the following day, on the final day of the festival. Their second performance was filmed, and Joplin, in a thigh-length gray cotton dress with baggy sleeves and matching tights, draped with a necklace of colored beads, became the centerpiece

JANIS JOPLIN'S INFLUENCES

★ Bessie Smith
★ Odetta
★ Big Mama Thornton
(early 20th-century African-American blues singers)

★ Otis Redding
★ Ike and Tina Turner
(African-American soul singers)

★ Kris Kristofferson
(American country singer-songwriter)

Throughout her brief career, Janis Joplin searched for the perfect backup band. After starting with Big Brother and the Holding Company, Joplin moved on to work with other larger bands, including ones that featured horn sections.

of the movie *Monterey Pop*. An outcast whose high-school peers had thought her unattractive was now setting fashion trends for the counterculture. The documentary catapulted Joplin into instant superstardom—suddenly, she was one of the decade's top performers, alongside the Beatles, the Rolling Stones, Jimi Hendrix, and the Doors.

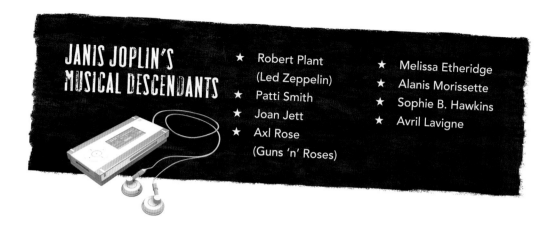

JANIS JOPLIN'S MUSICAL DESCENDANTS

★ Robert Plant (Led Zeppelin)
★ Patti Smith
★ Joan Jett
★ Axl Rose (Guns 'n' Roses)
★ Melissa Etheridge
★ Alanis Morissette
★ Sophie B. Hawkins
★ Avril Lavigne

Immediately, Big Brother and the Holding Company were signed to a record contract. The offer was made personally by Clive Davis, the president of Columbia Records, who rushed backstage moments after the band's first performance of "Ball and Chain." But nothing Joplin would record ever surpassed her performance that Saturday afternoon in June 1967—the day when it mattered the most.

Since Then

Joplin was alive for only three more years following the Monterey Pop Festival. Her life between the summer of 1967 and October 1970 was equal parts triumph and tragedy. Big Brother and the Holding Company's 1968 album, *Cheap Thrills*, was very successful, introducing Joplin's extraordinary singing to a worldwide audience. The band toured extensively and Joplin became known as one of the most electrifying live performers in the world.

However, more and more she felt the band was holding her back musically. She briefly formed a soul and blues band, the Kozmic Blues Band, with a full horn section. Though their album got good reviews and sold well, Joplin never got comfortable with the players. Less than a year later, she put together a new group, the Full Tilt Boogie Band.

This group was probably Joplin's best backing band. They accompanied her on a train tour across Canada in mid-1970. Joplin and the Full Tilt

During Joplin's three years in the spotlight, the media focused almost as much attention on her personal life as on her music. There were frequent reports of her public drunkenness and drug problems, and speculation about her affairs with stars such as Jimi Hendrix, Kris Kristofferson, and Jim Morrison.

musicians were almost finished recording another album, *Pearl*, when she died in the fall of 1970. *Pearl* was released after her death.

What killed Janis Joplin? She used to say she preferred a short life of excess to what she thought of as the only alternative: getting old and bored while watching TV. She couldn't imagine anything in between. Years before, she'd started drinking and partying to rebel. But she now found herself hooked. To the end of her life, Joplin was lonely. Some say that she may have been clinically depressed. She avoided her anxieties through drinking and drug use, and her success allowed her to behave without restrictions.

The official cause of her death was a drug overdose—late one night, alone in an LA hotel room, she injected herself with some unexpectedly strong heroin. But for years, Joplin had been abusing her body. Only 27 at the time of her death, she wasn't a healthy woman.

Joplin is a classic example of a rocker who lived fast and died too young. Nobody could have survived long at her pace, on and off the stage. She burned herself out spectacularly in public. In the process, she gave the world three great albums, countless amazing concerts, and haunting memories for anyone lucky enough to have seen her in June of the summer of love.

In Brief

Jimi Hendrix is the most important guitar player in rock history. During his three years in the spotlight, he revolutionized how the electric guitar is played. His unequaled style and technique are still the greatest influence on modern rock guitarists.

During his set at the Woodstock Festival, Hendrix played "The Star Spangled Banner." His unorthodox performance of the American national anthem was a bold musical step and a strong statement about America at the end of the '60s.

Jimi Hendrix
August 1969

Jimi Hendrix in performance.

The Band

Hendrix first became famous with a backing band called the Experience:

Noel Redding ★ bass guitar

Mitch Mitchell ★ drums

Later, he replaced Redding and Mitchell with other players, including an old friend, Billy Cox, on bass. Some of these other musicians played with him at Woodstock.

The Background

YOU WOULDN'T EXPECT A MUSICAL GENIUS to spring from the grim circumstances of Jimi Hendrix's childhood.

Called "Jimmy" until his mid-twenties, James Marshall Hendrix grew up poor, living with his father, Al, and younger brother Leon in Seattle, Washington. His mother Lucille drifted in and out of their lives, sometimes losing touch with her sons for long periods.

For Al and his two sons, life wasn't easy. Al did his best, working nights and trying to complete high school during the day. He was forced to put Leon into a foster home at one point. Meanwhile, Hendrix and his father lived in a rundown, two-room apartment, often splitting a can of beans and some Spam for dinner.

In 1958, Lucille died, when Hendrix was 15. Al would not allow his sons to attend the funeral. His mother's death and his father's strictness added to Hendrix's teenaged confusion. Playing the guitar helped him get through the hard times.

Hendrix had become interested in music at around 12 years of age when his father brought home a ukulele. Later, Hendrix bought himself an acoustic guitar for five dollars. As a left-hander, he had to turn the guitar around for it to feel natural. He and Al played at home sometimes, Jimmy on guitar and Al learning the saxophone or bass guitar.

By the time he was at Garfield High School in Seattle, Hendrix had an electric guitar and was teaching himself to play. Like most teenagers in the

Even with today's technology, top players still can't figure out how Hendrix produced the sounds he did using just a Fender Stratocaster, Marshall amps, and a few effects pedals. His approach was based on playing extremely loud, utilizing the full sonic potential of the electric guitar.

'50s, Hendrix loved the early rock and roll and rhythm and blues on the radio. He especially enjoyed Elvis Presley, Chuck Berry, and Ray Charles. Hendrix played guitar in a few bands during high school, performing a repertoire of early rock and pop music at dances and parties.

When he wasn't playing music, Hendrix hung out in cafés and on the street with a group of friends, getting into trouble. Eventually he was expelled from school; then he dropped out altogether. At 18, he was arrested for stealing and spent a week in jail. The judge agreed not to enforce the rest of Hendrix's sentence if he joined the army.

Jimi Hendrix took the sounds of warfare and incorporated them into his music.

WOODSTOCK MUSIC & ART FAIR
presents
AN AQUARIAN EXPOSITION
in
WHITE LAKE, N.Y.*

3 DAYS of PEACE & MUSIC

WITH

Joan Baez	Keef Hartley	The Band
	Canned Heat	Jeff Beck Group
Arlo Guthrie	Creedence Clearwater	Blood, Sweat and Tears
Tim Hardin	Grateful Dead	Joe Cocker
Richie Havens	Janis Joplin	Crosby, Stills and Nash
Incredible String Band	Jefferson Airplane	Jimi Hendrix
Ravi Shankar	Mountain	Iron Butterfly
Sly And The Family Stone	Quill	Ten Years After
Bert Sommer	Santana	Johnny Winter
Sweetwater	The Who	

FRI. AUG. 15   SAT. AUG. 16   SUN. AUG. 17

All programs subject to change without notice
*White Lake, Town of Bethel, Sullivan County, N.Y.

As Woodstock's attendance quickly soared beyond the wildest dreams of its organizers, efforts to collect tickets were abandoned. The largest festival of the decade was remarkably free of disaster, prompting a *New York Times* editorial to declare that it was "a phenomenon of innocence."

Hendrix spent the next year in the military as a paratrooper trainee, learning to jump from airplanes. While stationed at Fort Campbell in Kentucky, he began practicing guitar again. He experimented with different sounds on his instrument, incorporating the noises he heard in his surroundings—gunfire, explosions, the wind whistling into a parachute—into his playing.

After the army, Hendrix spent three years traveling back and forth across the country, playing guitar in more than a dozen bands backing up blues, rock, and soul musicians such as B.B. King and Little Richard. He didn't earn much and wasn't allowed to step into the spotlight, but he did learn a lot about music, performing, and how to entertain an audience. Although he had to play the same songs each night, he was slowly developing his own style—bending and stretching the guitar strings, using distortion, and getting unusual sounds out of his amplifier.

In 1965, Hendrix was living in New York. Bob Dylan's "Like a Rolling Stone" hit the radio that summer, and Hendrix fell in love with the song and with Dylan. Listening to Dylan convinced Hendrix that a great voice wasn't necessary to make great music. Soon he'd formed his own band, Jimmy James and the Blue Flames. They found work in New York clubs, and it was here that Hendrix would finally get a big break.

The word began to spread that there was a new guitarist who did amazing things on his instrument. Mike Bloomfield, one of the hottest guitar players in the country, had this to say after seeing the young phenom play:

THE ELECTRIC GUITAR

Without the electric guitar, rock music wouldn't have been possible. And rock music, in its turn, has elevated the electric guitar to become the world's most glamorous instrument.

Electric guitars allow players to go beyond what's written down in a song, adding feedback, distortion, sustained notes and vibrating pitch. Foot pedals that change the sound are often used between the guitar and the amplifier.

Electric guitars date back to the '30s, when Leo Fender began producing them for big-band guitarists who wanted to be heard above all the other instruments. One of his first models was called the Fender Telecaster; twenty years later Fender produced the Stratocaster. Both these guitars, with more modern body design and sophisticated electronics, became very popular with guitarists in the '60s—and still are. The "Strat"

has been the number-one guitar of players such as Buddy Holly, Jimi Hendrix, and Eric Clapton, while the Telecaster's sharp, twangy sound has made it a perfect choice for country-rock.

The other big name in electric guitars is Gibson. This company started churning out its signature model in the '50s—the Gibson Les Paul. It was named after guitarist and inventor Les Paul, who helped create some of the guitar's features, such as its powerful electronic pickups and heavy body. The Gibson Les Paul is great for hard rock and has been used by Jimmy Page and Neil Young, among others.

"Hendrix knew who I was and that day, in front of my eyes, he burned me to death... H-bombs were going off, guided missiles were flying... I didn't even want to pick up a guitar for the next year." Another impressed observer was Chas Chandler, the former bass player with a popular British band, the Animals. He invited Hendrix to go back to England with him, and promised to make him a star.

The Set-up

Within a week of arriving in London, Hendrix, just 23, had jammed with some of the city's hottest musicians. He'd played for members of the Beatles and the Who and for Eric Clapton. All of them shared Clapton's view that Hendrix was "incredible." Very soon, Hendrix was offered concert bookings, first in Paris, then back in England. Chas Chandler, by now Hendrix's manager, quickly put together a backing band. He hired Noel Redding on bass and Mitch Mitchell as the drummer, and encouraged Jimmy to change the spelling of his name. The Jimi Hendrix Experience was born.

The Experience stunned audiences. No one had ever seen a guitarist play the way Hendrix did. His Fender Stratocaster screamed and wailed, an extension of his body as he commanded the stage, dressed like a gypsy in bright colors and scarves. He was exotic, fashionable, and sexy. And he was the best musician anyone had ever heard.

In early 1967, the Experience's first single, "Hey Joe," was released. It was followed by one of Hendrix's own tunes, the psychedelic, distortion-soaked "Purple Haze." As the Experience became one of England's most popular bands, the group's third single, "The Wind Cries Mary" (another Hendrix original) was released. In May, came their first album, *Are You Experienced*. Around this time, Hendrix's stage show became even more theatrical. He would sometimes smash guitars, destroy amplifiers, and even lay his guitar down on the stage and set it on fire while Noel Redding and Mitch Mitchell pounded out a groove.

BEST ALBUMS

★ Are You Experienced (1967)

★ Axis: Bold as Love (1968)

★ Electric Ladyland (1968)

★ Smash Hits (1969) [compilation of hits from Hendrix's first three albums]

★ Band of Gypsys (1970) [live album]

In eight months, Jimi Hendrix had become the most exciting new rock star in Europe. It was only a matter of time before he conquered America. Paul McCartney helped by persuading the organizers of 1967's Monterey Pop Festival to put the Jimi Hendrix Experience on the bill.

At Monterey, Jimi Hendrix went onstage after an explosive set by the Who had left the audience drained. But with an even more dynamic performance, Hendrix and the Experience revived the crowd and ended their show with the most lasting image of the whole festival: Hendrix crouched in front of his guitar, coaxing flames from it as it burned. "When Jimi left the stage," wrote the *L.A. Times* music critic, "he had graduated from rumor to legend."

Now Hendrix began living the life of a rock star. He hung out in New York with other famous musicians; he lived in expensive hotels and showed up at clubs unannounced to jam with bands; and he gradually increased his use of drugs such as cocaine and LSD. When he wasn't playing, he was partying. Soon, he was seen everywhere, surrounded by friends and admirers. He had lots of girlfriends, many of them models and celebrities themselves.

But with fame came problems. Hendrix disliked the pressure of having his every move watched and reported by the media. He was also frustrated

In rock music, "feedback" is created when an instrument—usually an electric guitar—is turned up loud and held close to the amplifier it's plugged into. If the amp is also turned up loud, the guitar strings will continue to vibrate after being played, and sonic "overtones," or related pitches, will come from the speaker. Rock guitarists use feedback to sustain notes and to add dramatic, unearthly sounds to their playing.

at having to live up to his audience's expectations. Because he'd built his early reputation with the help of flashy tricks like playing guitar with his teeth and behind his back, as well as the smashing and torching of his instruments, crowds came to expect these things whenever he played. But Hendrix had always been very serious about his music, and now he resented people's demands for wild showmanship.

He was also ready to move beyond his old, crowd-pleasing hits. His definition of a successful performance wasn't necessarily based on

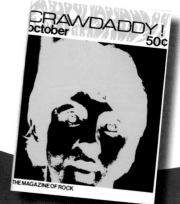

ROCK MUSIC MAGAZINES

In the mid-'60s, rock fans finally got their very own magazines, full of articles about the bands and personalities they loved.

The trend started in the US. Launched in 1966, *Crawdaddy!* was the first magazine devoted exclusively to rock music. *Rolling Stone* and *Creem* soon followed. In the UK, *Melody Maker* and *New Musical Express* (*NME*) were equally popular.

Many of today's most respected music writers got their start at American rock magazines.

Unlike others, *Rolling Stone* became more than a music magazine. Founded in San Francisco, it reflected the counterculture's attitudes about politics and social issues as well as featuring articles on other entertainment such as movies and literature.

By the end of the decade, the most popular magazines were highly influential.

Their album and concert reviews could affect a band's sales and concert attendance. Fans debated the critics' opinions and devoured the feature interviews with their favorite musicians. Music-industry professionals depended on charts tracking sales and radio airplay (like those in *Billboard* magazine) to measure their artists' success.

Today there are more music magazines than ever. Some of the early publications are gone, but others—like *Rolling Stone*—are still going strong. Newer titles such as *Spin, Mojo,* and *Q* give most fans what they want, while specialty magazines such as *Guitar Player* and *Modern Drummer* cater to musicians.

how the crowd responded. "If we're not laying down anything and they're screaming and hollering and thinking that's good, well then that makes you feel bad," he told an interviewer in London.

He hoped to interest audiences in his newer, more experimental songs. They were longer and less pop-oriented than the earlier hits. In 1968, he spent months at the Record Plant recording studio in New York finishing the Experience's third album, *Electric Ladyland*.

During this period he really became a perfectionist. He spent hours tuning and re-tuning guitars, experimenting with effects, and arguing about parts with Redding and Mitchell. He even insisted on playing some of the bass parts himself. His erratic work habits and autocratic ways created problems within the group, and Chas Chandler quit as manager and producer. Toward the end of the year, Redding and Mitchell got tired of their second-rate status in the band and decided to leave as well.

In the meantime, though, the *Electric Ladyland* album and its first single, a cover of Bob Dylan's "All Along the Watchtower," were released to great success in the fall of 1968. Critics and fans loved the extravagant double album that, more than anything previous, showed how much Jimi Hendrix, at 25 years of age, could do with an electric guitar. *Rolling Stone* magazine named him its "Performer of the Year" for 1968.

But during one of his performances the following year, he would show just how expressive his electric guitar could be.

Hendrix was very concerned with the sound of his records. To achieve greater control, he had a high-tech recording studio built to his own demanding specifications. When it was finished in 1970, Hendrix's Electric Lady Studios in New York allowed him unlimited time to experiment with sounds and re-record songs until he was finally satisfied. It's ironic that Hendrix never got a chance to release an album recorded at his own studio.

The Main Event

When Jimi Hendrix decided to make the US national anthem a part of his repertoire, his choice was seen as a political act. Though Hendrix wasn't overtly political, he was aware of the profound ideological rifts between the conservative, older generation and his own age group. He told a New York journalist, "The walls are crumbling and the establishment doesn't want to let go." In the '60s, amid social unrest, many Americans saw "The Star Spangled Banner" as a powerful symbol of the nation and the values they had fought to protect. All Americans knew their anthem note-for-note—but no one had ever heard it the way Hendrix played it.

He had performed "The Star Spangled Banner" at European concerts over the winter of 1968–1969. In March he recorded it—four minutes of every Hendrix sound imaginable woven into the song's familiar melody. But when he brought it out again in concert the following month in Texas,

Unlike guitar players before him, or even after, Hendrix had a gift for controlling feedback, distortion, and electronic effects.

there was a riot. So Hendrix knew exactly what he was doing when he launched into it onstage at the biggest rock concert ever—Woodstock.

Hendrix and his new band were the headliners; scheduled to perform last at the festival. By this point in his career, Hendrix was *always* the headliner; nobody wanted to have to entertain an audience after Hendrix's lethal combination of virtuosity, sexual charisma, and pyrotechnics. Backing Hendrix was a new band, Gypsy Sun and Rainbows: Mitch Mitchell back on drums, Hendrix's army buddy Billy Cox on bass, plus a rhythm guitarist and two percussionists.

Because of delays, Hendrix and his band didn't actually take the stage at Woodstock until Monday morning, after many of the half-million fans had already left, exhausted from a weekend of music, drugs, rain, and mud.

Hendrix too had been awake for days, doing drugs and jamming with his band. But he came on stage enthusiastically, dressed flamboyantly as always, this time in a white leather-fringed jacket hung with beads, a purple headband, and jewelery hanging off his bare chest. The band kicked off a set with a lot of new material they'd been working on—hard rock and blues, tinged with jazz and African elements. Some pieces were extended jams, while others were the hits that people knew. Then, near the end of his show, Hendrix looked out at the huge crowd, and with the rest of the band momentarily quiet, coaxed from his Stratocaster the first few notes of the one song everyone recognized instantly.

"The Star Spangled Banner" howled out of the massive speaker system. Hendrix's guitar, amplified to the sonic level of a fighter jet, tore across the field, bombarding the 60,000 fans with an arsenal of musical violence. Between the notes of the anthem, Hendrix simulated the sound of warfare. Behind him, the band added to the assault with sound effects of

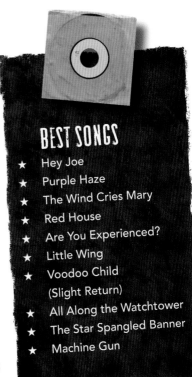

BEST SONGS

★ Hey Joe
★ Purple Haze
★ The Wind Cries Mary
★ Red House
★ Are You Experienced?
★ Little Wing
★ Voodoo Child
   (Slight Return)
★ All Along the Watchtower
★ The Star Spangled Banner
★ Machine Gun

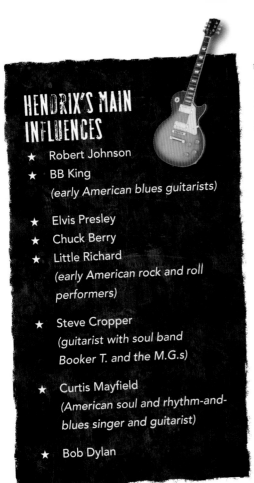

HENDRIX'S MAIN INFLUENCES

★ Robert Johnson
★ BB King
(early American blues guitarists)

★ Elvis Presley
★ Chuck Berry
★ Little Richard
(early American rock and roll performers)

★ Steve Cropper
(guitarist with soul band Booker T. and the M.G.s)

★ Curtis Mayfield
(American soul and rhythm-and-blues singer and guitarist)

★ Bob Dylan

their own. Hendrix pulled out all the stops that morning: he wrung every note, every scream, every explosion possible from his guitar and tortured amps. In his hands, the anthem became a requiem for the ideals of peace and brotherhood, trampled under the racial violence, protests, and foreign wars of American society in the late '60s. As the song drew to a close, leaving everyone stunned by its power and passion, Hendrix slid straight into the chunky intro to "Purple Haze." After the set, he walked offstage and collapsed. Woodstock was over and the tumultuous decade was drawing to a close.

Since Then

Interviewed after the festival, Jimi Hendrix was asked to explain his interpretation of "The Star Spangled Banner." He said, "I don't know, man, all I did was play it. I'm American so I played it." He famously told TV host Dick Cavett, "I thought it was beautiful."

A little over a year later, Hendrix was dead. He was yet another casualty of the rock-star lifestyle, dead because of too much success, too much money, too much pressure, and too much drinking and drug use. Hendrix's life ended in London at the apartment of one of his girlfriends. The doctors said he had choked on his own vomit after taking too many sleeping pills—but Hendrix had been abusing his body for many years by the time he died. He seemed destined for some kind of catastrophe. Like Janis Joplin and Jim Morrison, Jimi Hendrix was only 27 at the time of his death.

It's likely that, if he had lived, Hendrix would have continued to grow

WOODSTOCK

The largest rock festival ever at the time, Woodstock took place on August 15, 16, and 17, 1969. It was originally supposed to be held in the small town of Woodstock, New York, but local residents objected, and the concert was moved miles away to a field owned by a farmer, Max Yasgur.

Some of the world's most popular musicians performed at the festival. Highlights included sets by the Who, Creedence Clearwater Revival, Janis Joplin, Joan Baez, Crosby, Stills, Nash, and Young, the Grateful Dead, Jefferson Airplane, and Jimi Hendrix.

Woodstock's slogan was "three days of peace and music," and it lived up to the name. Although there were as many as 500,000 people in attendance, instead of the expected 50,000, and although it rained much of the weekend, turning the site into a huge mud pit, everyone co-existed peacefully. Fans slept on the ground and shared food, alcohol, and marijuana. People took off their clothes and danced in the rain. Woodstock has come to symbolize the hippie vision and many felt it was the high point of the '60s.

as a musician, branching out in revolutionary directions. He was already moving toward more jazz- and funk-oriented, experimental music, and with the completion of his own studio, was ready to spend more time recording the otherworldly sounds he heard in his head. His death cut short what should have been a long and brilliant career.

Hendrix's music still sounds as raw and powerful as ever. Rock guitarists all over the world have said they've learned most from Hendrix. Like only a few other classic rock performers, Jimi Hendrix lives on in music long after passing away.

In Brief

After ten years of working hard and getting nowhere, Creedence Clearwater Revival blazed onto the scene in 1969 with a timeless song called "Proud Mary." They were from the San Francisco area, but their hard-driving roots-rock distinguished them from the many psychedelic "acid" rock groups around them.

They established themselves as America's hottest singles band, releasing a string of hits that dominated rock radio for the next three years. Creedence Clearwater Revival's story is a testament to how dedication, discipline, and a solid sense of identity can take a band to the top of the music world.

Creedence Clearwater Revival 1969

The "average guys" of Creedence Clearwater Revival: Doug Clifford, Tom Fogerty, John Fogerty, and Stu Cook.

The Band

Creedence Clearwater Revival (also known as Creedence, or just CCR) had the same lineup for most of their career.

John Fogerty ★ lead vocals, lead guitar, occasional organ, saxophone, other instruments

Tom Fogerty ★ rhythm guitar

Stu Cook ★ bass guitar

Doug Clifford ★ drums

John Fogerty wrote almost all their songs.

The Background

THE FOUR MEMBERS OF CCR grew up together in El Cerrito, a sleepy suburb of Berkeley, California. Though only 20 miles from San Francisco's Haight-Ashbury district, El Cerrito might as well have been on another planet given the difference between the two communities. Haight-Ashbury was the center of the '60s "counterculture" movements in politics, sexual freedom, and drugs—especially LSD or "acid."

The fact that CCR stayed true to their average, middle-class hometown roots is what set them apart from so many other American rock bands of the late '60s.

John Fogerty and his older brother Tom were part of a family of five boys. As a teenager, John spent hours in the basement learning to play the guitar. At high school, he formed a band with classmates Doug Clifford and Stu Cook. They called themselves the Blue Velvets and began playing at local dances and parties.

Meanwhile, Tom sang with a band that had signed a record contract but split up before releasing any music. He then joined the Blue Velvets; because he could sing, he was a welcome addition. In 1961, the new four-piece Blue Velvets released their first songs with a local record company.

They got some radio airplay on small northern California stations, but by 1962, the band had been dropped by the company and was looking for a new contract.

For five years—from 1963 to 1968—the band struggled. They played anywhere they could, and each member worked a day job just to make ends meet. By this time, Tom was already married with a new family to support. When John and Clifford were drafted into the army, the Blue Velvets had to disband temporarily.

"Born on the Bayou" borrows some of its mythical, "swampy" imagery from two Mississippi blues musicians, Howlin' Wolf and Muddy Waters.

The band got a break when a small San Francisco jazz label, Fantasy Records, signed them up. But the deal came with conditions. The company billed them as the Golliwogs and made them wear uniforms and white wigs. They weren't too happy, but they needed the work.

A few changes improved the band—Cook switched from piano to bass and John started singing—but by 1967 the band was at a crossroads. Three of them now had families to support. It was a make-or-break moment.

John told the group they needed to commit fully to music if they wanted to succeed. So Tom quit his job with the power company and dipped

In his early teens, John Fogerty bought an electric guitar and amplifier with money he earned delivering newspapers. As a child, he imagined playing the music he loved: the blues, rhythm-and-blues songs such as those of Ray Charles, and the rock and roll music of Bo Diddley and Chuck Berry.

into his family savings. Cook sold his new car to help pay band bills. Even with these sacrifices, times were tough. Tom said, "Two or three months before our first album, we had exactly two dollars in our common checking account."

Late in the year, luck finally changed when Fantasy was bought by Saul Zaentz, the company's sales manager. He renegotiated the band's contract and encouraged them to change their name. They used the first name of a friend, Credence, changing the spelling to "Creedence"; took a phrase from a beer commercial ("clear water"); and added "Revival" as a sign that they intended to do something different: something that sounded like yesterday's music played in a new way.

With a new name, new equipment bought by Zaentz, and a new leader—John—they recorded their first album as CCR in early 1968. John knew what he wanted to hear: "A great record has four things, in this order: title, the sound, the words, and then the last thing, which all great rock and roll records have: a really great guitar riff."

Their first hit was a version of rock standard, "Suzie Q," which reached number 11 on the national radio charts that summer. Soon, CCR was playing all over the US, sharing stages with more established bands that often played much longer, less-focused songs than John and his bandmates did.

But CCR was about to take rock music back to basics.

Despite all the hard work during the mid-'60s, the band wasn't very good. Looking back, John later admitted, "Stu only knew three notes on the bass at the time. Tom played one string on the guitar, and then I filled in all the other instruments..." Clifford agreed: "The reason it took us so long to make it is simple," he said. "When we started, we were terrible."

SINGLES AND SALES

In the '60s—long before CDs or MP3s—nearly all music was sold in two ways: as long-playing albums (LPs), which contained around ten songs; and as singles (also called 45s), which typically featured the most popular song from the album on the "A" side, and another on the reverse.

The record company would often listen to the band's new songs and choose the best candidate for a hit single. Then they'd release it before the full album was released. It was intended partly as a kind of tease to maximize sales: although some fans bought only singles, many who liked the single would go back and spend more money on the album when it was later released. Other tracks on the album could be longer or more experimental, but, ideally, a single had to be "catchy"—instantly likable, a tune that would stick in people's heads after they heard it for the first time on the radio. By releasing singles before the album, record companies also benefited from the advance promotion of radio play.

Record companies would commonly put out more than one single from an album. Occasionally, both the "A" and "B" (front and back) sides of a 45 would be hit singles. Companies also generated more sales by "backing" a single with another song not included on the album. This gave fans extra incentive to buy the single *and* the album.

Finally, record companies released "greatest hits" albums many years into a band's career, or after the band had split up. These contained the hit singles from all of the band's albums collected on one LP and augmented by a few longer album tracks, unreleased songs, or live performances. As always, serious fans would spend money to make sure they didn't miss anything.

Sales of 45s got the cash registers ringing.

Rollin'

John Fogerty had been waiting 10 years for his chance, and now he was ready. By 1969, John's songwriting skills were at their peak. He began crafting short, catchy tunes—perfect radio singles with a strong beat, memorable guitar lines, and choruses that stuck in people's minds. He also wrote very fast: within 18 months, CCR would have an astonishing 20 songs make the Top 100 singles chart.

The string started early in 1969. "Proud Mary" was released, backed with "Born on the Bayou." John knew he'd at last discovered something special, both in musical style and content. Both songs draw on the myths of the Deep South, with its dark, mysterious swamps, magic, and the Mississippi River. John had always been fascinated with this place, reading the stories about Tom Sawyer and Huck Finn when he was a boy, and later, listening to the black blues that came from the South. He had always dreamed of living there.

For many, civil rights leader Martin Luther King was a visionary as well as a prophet of non-violence. When he was assassinated in 1968, riots broke out and the whole nation mourned. The disasters described in "Bad Moon Rising," released by Creedence Clearwater Revival the next year, echoed the troubled times.

The straightforward blues-country-rockabilly sound that CCR had nailed with "Suzie Q" was a perfect musical setting for John's lyrics about swamp magic and riverboats. "Proud Mary," with its unforgettable chorus, reached number two on the charts. It was then featured on CCR's next album, *Bayou Country*. By this point, most Americans assumed the band was from somewhere in the South, probably Louisiana. Some people even thought they were black.

They kept up the momentum by recording two more songs within a few months: "Bad Moon Rising" and "Lodi." In "Bad Moon Rising," John sang of hurricanes, earthquakes, and death. It fit the country's mood perfectly. Americans believed the song was a comment on current events—the recent assassinations of civil rights leader Martin Luther King and presidential candidate Robert Kennedy, the riots and protests all over the country, and the continuing war in Vietnam.

By the end of the summer, the next album, *Green River*, was released featuring these two songs. The album was again influenced by the culture of the South. Before the year was out, a third album appeared, *Willy and the Poor Boys*. It was perhaps their best of the year.

Between 1963 and 1968, CCR went from terrible to "tight" (well-rehearsed and able to play without mistakes). Once in the studio, they recorded very quickly. They often recorded most of an album within a week, for less than $2,000 in studio time. By '60s standards, CCR's efficiency was rare. By today's standards, with albums taking years to record and costing hundreds of thousands of dollars, it seems impossible.

SUCCESS, NOT EXCESS

CCR didn't fit the stereotype of late '60s rock bands. They looked like average guys—for example, they're wearing jeans and checked work shirts on the album cover of *Green River*. They also stayed away from the typical rock-star lifestyle of excess. There are no stories of them wrecking hotel rooms or driving motorcycles into swimming pools. On the road, they didn't have wild parties waist-deep in women and drugs.

John in particular was firm about his beliefs. "I was anti-drug, which was a weird stance to be taking then," he said later. He'd tried marijuana, but hadn't enjoyed it. The band never performed while drunk or stoned, and didn't have much interest in the '60s drug culture.

In fact, John didn't even enjoy the biggest rock festival of the decade. When CCR played at Woodstock in August 1969, they went onstage at 3 a.m., right after the Grateful Dead. As the band got further into an energetic set, John grew frustrated. Most of the audience was asleep in the mud or too stoned to respond to the music. He later grew disillusioned with the festival and all it represented, and refused to allow CCR's performance to be included on the *Woodstock* film or album. He said they hadn't played well enough.

In spite of their rejection of trendy fashions and ideas—or perhaps because of it—CCR earned fans across all tastes, races, and social brackets.

John's writing on this album showed a new side: direct social criticism. Its strongest statement was "Fortunate Son," a flat-out rocker about President Richard Nixon and his government's Vietnam War policy. John took aim at the privileged few who made the big decisions but didn't risk their own lives. The song took less than half an hour to write, which he explained by saying, "Richard Nixon is a great inspiration." It was immediately recognized as one of rock's strongest anti-Vietnam War songs. In years since, it's been played at anti-war demonstrations every time the US launches a military campaign.

Republican Richard M. Nixon, seen here with musician Ray Charles, was president of the US from early 1969 until 1974. He was in office during a turbulent time: the first moon landing, the continuation of the Vietnam War, and the bombing of Cambodia all took place during the Nixon administration. He was often contrasted with John F. Kennedy, the young, glamorous Democratic president tragically assassinated in 1963. To young people, Nixon symbolized everything old-fashioned and hypocritical about the "establishment."

Willy and the Poor Boys reached the top ten on the charts and two of the songs were hits—a spectacular way to end the year.

After so many years of hard work, everything seemed to gel surprisingly quickly. In less than a year, CCR recorded three albums full of songs that sounded totally different than most rock music in late-'60s America. Their music appealed to everyone: fans of hard rock, country, blues, '50s rock and roll, and black music. No band before or since had such a diverse audience.

Maybe CCR was able to reach so many people because they were so earthy. They had no flashy gimmicks or costumes, and they didn't pretend to be anything but four guys from El Cerrito who loved old blues and rock music. Though they eventually sold more than 100 million records, nobody in CCR,

BEST SONGS

★ Suzie Q
★ Born on the Bayou
★ Proud Mary
★ Green River
★ Bad Moon Rising
★ Down on the Corner
★ Fortunate Son
★ Travelin' Band
★ Who'll Stop the Rain?
★ Have You Ever Seen the Rain?

THE WATERGATE SCANDAL

Richard Nixon's time as president was finished a year after the last soldiers returned from Vietnam. He was implicated in a botched 1972 break-in at the rival Democratic Party headquarters at the Watergate building in Washington, DC.

Two White House officials, E. Howard Hunt and G. Gordon Liddy, organized the ill-fated break-in. The innocent-looking ChapStick tubes, pictured here, contain tiny hidden microphones and kept the organizers and burglars in contact during the break-in. They were later discovered in Hunt's White House office safe, and used as evidence.

Although there was no hard evidence that Nixon was directly involved in the crime, later investigations showed he'd tried to cover it up and had bribed government officials to stay quiet. When exposed, the Watergate affair became a massive scandal. Nixon was threatened with impeachment—being forced from office—and instead resigned in disgrace in August 1974.

624.0231 "Chapstick" Microphone #24.254

not even John Fogerty, ever became a celebrity to the degree of Jim Morrison or Janis Joplin. CCR remained anonymous, keeping their private lives private.

But the story of CCR is also about personalities—specifically, the rivalry and bad feelings that arose among brothers and friends. Less than four years after the first CCR album, the group was gone, and these former bandmates would spend most of the following 30 years blaming each other for what went wrong.

Since Then

The end didn't come right away. In fact, in 1970, CCR released *Cosmo's Factory*, which became their most popular album ever. It included a folk-rock tune called "Who'll Stop the Rain?"—another song about the continuing war in Vietnam. It, like "Fortunate Son" and another new track, "Run through the Jungle," became forever associated with the antiwar movement in the US.

John's creativity was still running high, and he was able to write two or three hit songs over a weekend. Late in 1970, another album was released. Called *Pendulum*, this turned out to be CCR's last great record. Its best song was also its saddest: "Have You Ever Seen the Rain?" While most fans believed the song was another comment on the state of the world, it was in fact a personal statement from John about the coming break-up of CCR.

Ever since John had taken control of the band in 1968, there had been arguments about his leadership. Despite their success, the other members continued to question John's decisions. Cook, a business major in college, wanted to take over some of CCR's business dealings, which John had always run. Tom and Doug Clifford also wanted an equal part in songwriting and singing.

Early in 1971, things began to fall apart. Tom quit, unable to continue taking orders from his younger brother. Tom announced plans to launch a solo career, and the rest of the band made a public statement wishing him well.

John, Stu Cook, and Doug Clifford continued for another year as a trio. They toured, continuing to get good reviews for their live performances, and then entered the studio to make another record. This time, John gave the others the full democracy they'd demanded: he asked the two of them to write and sing one-third of the album each. The album that resulted, *Mardi Gras*, was a failure, according to most critics. *Rolling Stone* magazine called it "Fogerty's revenge" and said it was the worst album ever from a major rock band.

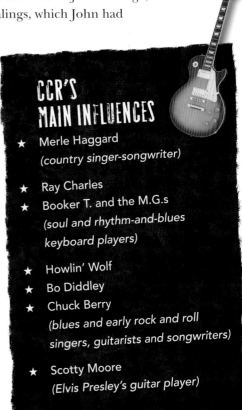

CCR'S MAIN INFLUENCES

★ Merle Haggard
(country singer-songwriter)

★ Ray Charles
★ Booker T. and the M.G.s
(soul and rhythm-and-blues keyboard players)

★ Howlin' Wolf
★ Bo Diddley
★ Chuck Berry
(blues and early rock and roll singers, guitarists and songwriters)

★ Scotty Moore
(Elvis Presley's guitar player)

COUNTRY MUSIC

Rock and roll owes a heavy debt to classic country music from the '40s and '50s.

Country songs combined stories—about lost love, drinking, and money problems—with catchy tunes, hot guitar or fiddle playing, and a danceable rhythm. They were working people's songs, music that mostly rural folks could relate to without the benefit of formal training or education. For the most part, country stars stayed away from the flash and glamor of other entertainers, preferring a down-to-earth, rural image.

Classic country originated in the '30s, with Jimmie Rodgers and the Carter family. They in turn influenced Hank Williams, Sr., country music's dominant figure. Williams was only 29 when he died in 1953, but his singing and songwriting set the standard for the country singers who followed—Johnny Cash, Waylon Jennings, Merle Haggard, and Willie Nelson. All used guitar, bass, drums, and piano on most records, sometimes adding fiddle and pedal steel guitar.

Through the '50s, country produced a speeded-up offshoot called "rockabilly." Its stars were Bill Haley, Elvis Presley, Carl Perkins, and Buddy Holly. They took the final steps toward rock and roll. Later bands like the Beatles and the Who combined the energy of rockabilly with the intensity of blues and the beat of rhythm and blues—and rock music was born.

Later, the Rolling Stones, Bob Dylan, CCR, and Crosby, Stills, Nash, and Young would take the sounds of classic country and incorporate them in their own songs.

★ *Bayou Country* (1969)

★ *Green River* (1969)

★ *Willy and the Poor Boys* (1969)

★ *Cosmo's Factory* (1970)

★ *The Long Road Home* (2005) [compilation of CCR hits and John Fogerty's solo songs]

After the embarrassment of *Mardi Gras*, the final split came in 1972—the result of hard feelings on all sides. The former friends were now enemies, and once they'd broken up, John tried to avoid communicating with Cook, Clifford, and even his brother Tom.

John quickly recorded a solo country record. He sang and played all the instruments, but concealed his own involvement by releasing it under the name "Blue Ridge Rangers." Another solo album followed in 1975, after which he stopped producing music for a decade due to legal problems with his Fantasy Records contract. When these were finally resolved, he released the album *Centerfield* in 1985. Once again, he not only wrote all the songs, but also played all the instruments. It was an immediate success.

Meanwhile, Cook and Clifford continued to work together, occasionally playing with Tom, with mediocre success. In the late '80s, Tom battled with AIDS, which he had contracted from a blood transfusion during an operation on his back. He died in 1990, only 48 years old. He and John never really reconciled, though John did visit him before he passed away.

Finally, in 1993, CCR was inducted into the Rock and Roll Hall of Fame. What should have been a happy occasion instead turned into another opportunity for the three surviving members to take shots at each other. The band was invited to perform at the ceremony, but John refused to play with the others, playing instead with Bruce Springsteen and other musicians. Clifford and Cook were furious at John's betrayal. After that incident, it's hard to imagine a CCR reunion ever happening.

CCR'S MUSICAL DESCENDANTS

* Bob Seger
* Bruce Springsteen
* Tom Petty & the Heartbreakers
* John Mellencamp
* the Black Crowes
* Steve Earle
* Blue Rodeo
* the Tragically Hip

Despite the bitterness among the musicians themselves, today their music remains as popular as ever. Groups all over the world still spice up their repertoire with "Proud Mary," "Bad Moon Rising," and other CCR songs. And on any night, on any stage where there's a bar band struggling through its set, everything suddenly sounds fine and the dance floor fills up when the musicians launch into one of those timeless hits from CCR.

In Brief

By 1969, the Rolling Stones were calling themselves the "World's Greatest Rock and Roll Band," and were doing their best to live up to the name.

At the Altamont Speedway, not far from San Francisco, they put on a massive free concert on December 6. With the Hell's Angels motorcycle gang as concert security, however, the show turned ugly. Peace, love, and togetherness—values so important to young people during the '60s—seemed to disappear, as the decade itself came to a close.

The Rolling Stones
December 1969

The Rolling Stones in performance:
Mick Taylor, Mick Jagger, Keith Richards,
Charlie Watts, and Bill Wyman

The Band

Here's who was in the Rolling Stones at the time:

Mick Jagger	★	lead vocals
Keith Richards	★	rhythm and lead guitar; backing and occasional lead vocals
Charlie Watts	★	drums
Mick Taylor	★	lead and electric slide guitar (Taylor had recently replaced Brian Jones, one of the original members)
Bill Wyman	★	bass guitar

Jagger has always written most Stones lyrics, with his co-leader Richards writing most of the music.

The Background

THE ROLLING STONES started out in London, England in the early '60s. Mick Jagger had already performed in bands at school, and Keith Richards was teaching himself to play guitar, spending hours listening to records. The two were soon in a blues band performing the songs they loved in London clubs. But the band didn't really click until Charlie Watts and Bill Wyman, both older and more experienced jazz players, were persuaded to join. Then they connected with Brian Jones, a gifted, charismatic musician who would guide the Stones through their first few years.

They took their name from the title of an old song by the legendary American blues singer Muddy Waters, paying their respects to the music that inspired them. Soon they were performing to packed houses. It was at this point that their first manager, Andrew Loog Oldham, realized that the Stones could be promoted as a darker, meaner alternative to the Beatles. Oldham got them their first recording contract in the summer of 1963.

The Stones' first records featured only "covers," the band's versions of other people's songs. But Oldham understood that future albums should feature their own music. He encouraged Jagger and Richards to develop

Keith Richards is considered by many as the best rhythm guitarist in rock. He strums his guitar as if it were a percussion instrument, establishing the groove in every song. He's also known for his unique sound, which he gets by tuning his guitar to "open" chords and sometimes removing the low E string, just like "Delta blues" guitarists did.

The *Apollo XI* mission of 1969 put a man on the moon for the first time, after several failed attempts over a decade and billions of dollars spent in trying. Here, the lunar module Eagle returns to the mother ship Columbia, with the Earth a tiny semi-circle in the distance. The miracle of the moon landing inspired a sense of awe and possibility in almost everyone who saw it.

their own songwriting skills. This strategy didn't take long to pay off. In 1965, the band broke through with "Satisfaction." Over the next few years, songs like "Get Off My Cloud," "As Tears Go By," "Mother's Little Helper," and "19th Nervous Breakdown" cemented their reputation as one of the premier bands of the '60s. From that point on, the hits kept coming.

A MEANER ALTERNATIVE

As the Stones made an impact on rock radio, their cocky, ironic songs dropped like bombs onto conservative British and American society. But the songs were only partly responsible for their notoriety. Unlike the early Beatles, who smiled and joked with the press, the Stones were the kind of guys mothers didn't want their daughters going out with. Jagger and Richards were among the first rock musicians to cultivate a dark, sensual image and use it to sell themselves and their music.

Every story that shocked the public added to the band's mythic status. At a time when pop stars were clean-cut and polite, the Stones wore their hair long and looked dirty. They had wild parties with famous actresses and models. Long before people had grown used to hearing about rock musicians breaking laws, the Stones made news headlines with drug possession charges. Throughout the second half of the '60s, the Stones embodied everything dangerous and sinister about rock and roll.

The Set-up

By the summer of 1969 the Beatles were close to breaking up. Bob Dylan had stopped touring. This left the Stones as the most popular band around.

But one thing bothered them: they hadn't performed at the huge Woodstock rock festival earlier in the year. They decided to stage their own "western Woodstock." Fans were thrilled. It would be a free celebration, bringing music and people together. The bill included popular west coast bands like Jefferson Airplane, Santana, and the Grateful Dead, as well as superstars Crosby, Stills, Nash, and Young. Jagger told the US media that they wanted to set "an example to the rest of America as to how one can behave in nice gatherings."

The festival got the band into the news—but for the wrong reason.

The Players

By the late '60s, the band belonged to Jagger and Richards. These two had met at preschool, then gone their separate ways. Over a decade later, a teenaged Richards was waiting for a train when he spotted Jagger. Richards was surprised to see his old friend carrying LPs under his arm, and amazed that Jagger's albums were the same old American blues and rhythm-and-blues records that obsessed Richards himself.

It was this music that bonded the teenagers. They had grown up in similar circumstances, were the same age, and, at least in the '60s, were musical soul mates. But as the Stones' career took flight, it became clear that Jagger and Richards were not similar.

Jagger was a born entertainer, at ease in the spotlight. He became the voice and most recognizable face of the band. He enjoyed glamor and celebrity, mixing comfortably with rich society. A former student at the London School of Economics, he evolved into a shrewd businessman, calculating every move the Stones made, carefully tending to his own image and the band's.

Richards, by contrast, was straight-ahead. The son of a factory worker, he was the most passionate about rock and roll, happier sitting with a guitar in his hands than socializing with the international jet set. He loved writing songs, rehearsing, and jamming, looking for that moment when everything would sound just as it did in his head. And, more than Jagger, Richards revered the old black blues musicians.

Jagger and Richards were like brothers. They shared a deep bond, but sometimes fought. They argued about songs, their performances, and how to market the band. Whenever Jagger pulled the band too far from its musical roots, Richards brought them back to their best material—earthy, blues-based rock and roll.

When the Rolling Stones appeared on the popular _Ed Sullivan Show_, the host was concerned about the sexual morality of their lyrics. Sullivan demanded that they change their hit song from "Let's Spend the Night Together" to "Let's Spend Some Time Together." The Stones, supposedly rock's bad boys, willingly obeyed.

The Concert

The sun had set over the Altamont Speedway, and the December night was chilly. There were almost 300,000 people waiting impatiently for the headline act. Many had been there all day, some since the night before. They had sat through many performances. Typical of most rock concerts in the '60s, a lot of drugs were going around. Some people had

MUDDY WATERS

McKinley Morganfield, a.k.a. Muddy Waters, was an African-American blues singer, guitarist, and songwriter. He was born in 1915 into a very poor Mississippi family. In his teens, he taught himself to play "Delta blues," first on harmonica and later on guitar. These songs were made for poor people just like Muddy: the music was raw and powerful, and the words reflected the poverty, lack of opportunity, and personal tragedy of their lives.

Later, Muddy moved to Chicago and formed his own bands. He was one of the first to play blues on electric guitar, and he became renowned for his strong "bottle-neck slide" guitar playing and his deep, emotional singing. From the late '40s onward he played live shows and made records with bands that always included outstanding players on bass, piano, and harmonica. He wrote many famous songs, such as "Rollin' Stone," from which Mick Jagger, Keith Richards, and Brian Jones took their band name.

By the time he died in 1983, Muddy Waters' brand of electric blues had evolved into rock and roll. He's considered a main influence by classic rock guitarists and songwriters, including Jimi Hendrix, Eric Clapton, Jimmy Page, and, of course, the Rolling Stones.

In the '60s, British radio stations played soft, "easy-listening" music. Black music from across the Atlantic Ocean captivated Jagger and Richards because it was different. American blues was meaner, with a heavy back beat and hard-hitting lyrics about real life.

taken too much and were freaking out, stripping off their clothes, screaming, and throwing things.

There were also problems with the site itself. The speedway was a huge, empty space in the middle of nowhere, without stands, bleachers, or seats. The stage was only a few feet high. Big video screens didn't exist in 1969, so for many fans, the performers weren't visible. What's more, there wasn't enough food or water, and there were almost no bathrooms.

Worst of all, "security" was being enforced by the most notorious and violent motorcycle gang in the world, the California chapter of the Hell's Angels. The Rolling Stones had hired them, reasoning that the Angels—big, aggressive men—could control the gathering better than the police or any private security company.

But it wasn't working. Throughout the day, as each new band had taken the stage and fans pressed forward, the Angels waded into the front rows to attack people with their heavy pool cues or rode their motorcycles through the crowd. The bands onstage pleaded again and again for peace and calm, but the violence continued.

Finally, long after sundown, the Rolling Stones appeared. A huge cheer rose from the dark. In the spotlight stood Jagger in black with a red cape and scarf, and Richards to his left in a red satin shirt.

BEST ALBUMS

★ Beggars Banquet (1968)
★ Let it Bleed (1969)
★ Sticky Fingers (1971)
★ Hot Rocks (greatest hits package from the '60s and early '70s)
★ Exile on Main Street (1972)

Jagger stepped up to the mike. "Ooh, babies," he said. "There's so many of you...just be cool down in front there, don't push around."

With that, the band launched into "Sympathy for the Devil." It was their latest and most notorious song. Many thought Jagger's lyrics promoted devil worship. When the band began playing at Altamont, the crowd responded immediately. Those near the front were almost climbing, or being shoved, right up onto the stage. Even Richards looked nervous.

The Angels attacked. Pool cues whistled through the air, bodies recoiled, and people fell away. Jagger turned to Richards, stopped the music, and spoke to the crowd. "Sisters and brothers, just cool out—everybody just cool out now, all right?"

The beatings stopped briefly. Then Watts' drums and Wyman's bass thundered to life once more. Jagger danced around crazily, pouting and

Last-minute complications meant that preparations for the free Rolling Stones concert at Altamont had to be rushed. The construction crew barely had time to build a low stage. The local Hell's Angels were hired to provide security, reputedly for $500 worth of beer.

BEST SONGS

- ★ (I Can't Get No) Satisfaction
- ★ Jumpin' Jack Flash
- ★ Sympathy for the Devil
- ★ Honky Tonk Women
- ★ Gimme Shelter
- ★ Brown Sugar
- ★ Wild Horses
- ★ Angie
- ★ It's Only Rock 'n' Roll
- ★ Start Me Up

grinning at the audience, ignoring the trouble that had begun again. Richards stood still, his face blank, fingers grinding out the chords.

The shoving and punching continued on and off for several minutes. When "Sympathy" ended, Jagger spoke to the crowd again. "Uh, people," he began. "Now, who's fighting, and what for?" Richards, obviously agitated, pointed to the crowd. "Either those cats cool it or we don't play," he added, to no one in particular.

This was as close as the Stones got to using their authority to stop the violence. They never stopped playing. Jagger may have been unaware of how bad the problems were; or he might have felt that the huge crowd was uncontrollable. They continued the show despite the violence.

As they launched into the next song, the Angels again cracked heads. When the song ended a few minutes later, all hell broke loose. A young black man in a flashy green suit swung across an open space in the crowd in front of Richards. He pulled a gun and began to raise it, but before he'd straightened his arm, an Angel jumped and stabbed him. The young man fell, bleeding.

The man was Meredith Hunter. Barely 18, he'd come to Altamont with his

"Gimme Shelter" is one of the Stones' most frightening and bleak songs, with its chorus about war, rape, and murder. It's on the album *Let it Bleed*, released on December 5, 1969—the day before Altamont.

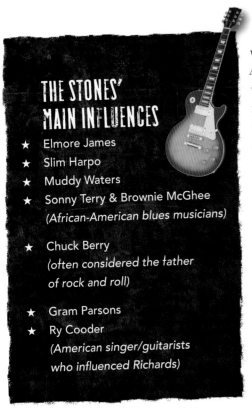

THE STONES' MAIN INFLUENCES

★ Elmore James
★ Slim Harpo
★ Muddy Waters
★ Sonny Terry & Brownie McGhee
(African-American blues musicians)

★ Chuck Berry
(often considered the father of rock and roll)

★ Gram Parsons
★ Ry Cooder
(American singer/guitarists who influenced Richards)

white girlfriend. Some accounts say that the Angels killed him because he was a black man with a white woman. But the documentary film of the concert, *Gimme Shelter*, clearly shows a gun in his hand before he was attacked. No one has ever explained why he had a gun, or why he chose to raise it toward the stage. The act cost him his life and made him the most famous rock-concert casualty ever.

Hunter was loaded into a helicopter and airlifted away, already dead. Onstage, the Rolling Stones kicked into "Street Fighting Man," perhaps hoping to prevent more trouble.

The next morning, thousands of young people returned to San Francisco. Few of them realized they'd witnessed the end of an era. Altamont itself didn't destroy the '60s values of peace and happiness, but it showed that a simple belief in togetherness could not protect people against the anger and violence of the world. The decade was over. The following years would see its ideals slowly replaced—in music and elsewhere—by self-interest and materialism. Altamont was the surest sign of this change.

Since Then

Not long after Altamont, and perhaps due to the pressures of superstardom, Richards descended into a decade-long battle with heroin addiction. Jagger effectively ran the band. By the late '70s, when Richards finally kicked his habit, he'd acquired a reputation as rock's greatest survivor.

In the meantime, the band put out some average albums with a few great songs sprinkled among them, including "Brown Sugar," "Angie," "Heartbreaker," and "It's Only Rock 'n' Roll." The Stones came back big

THE BIG DEAL ABOUT LONG HAIR

Today, we see so many different hairstyles (not to mention piercings and tattoos) that it's hard to imagine that long hair was once controversial.

As the '60s began, most young men had their hair cut just like their fathers did. The standard had been set decades previously, as reflected by the clean-cut look of stars such as Cary Grant and Frank Sinatra. Once Elvis Presley and James Dean came along, hair started to become a little longer, though only on top. In the '50s, a man's ears and neck still showed.

But there were changes coming, and rock musicians popularized the new style. By 1964, British bands, led by the Beatles, the Rolling Stones and the Who, were growing their hair longer; by 1967, many rock stars—and their fans—had hair that hung way past their ears, and over their shoulders. Parents were shocked: they disliked the Stones' haircuts as much as they did the music. For the older generation, the long hair was dirty and disrespectful. For the younger generation, long hair symbolized rebellion against old-fashioned values.

In the late '60s, the hippies' hair was waist length, and was often adorned with flowers and colorful headbands. Young people who kept their hair short were often criticized by their peers for being conservative or "square."

It was only in the late '70s when punk rock and new wave music became popular that hairstyles changed again. Since then, musicians—and fans—haven't been tied to any specific style. Now, you can find heavy-metal singers with buzz-cuts and rappers with long dreadlocks…and hairstyles aren't controversial anymore.

in 1978 with the album *Some Girls* and its catchy single, "Miss You." Shortly after that came the song that still opens Stones shows to this day, the unforgettable "Start Me Up," from the album *Tattoo You.*

Their "bad boy" reputation shadowed their musical success throughout the '70s and '80s. Even their record covers occasionally created problems. The release of *Beggar's Banquet* was held up almost half a year because the

In 2005, a California court finally closed the Meredith Hunter case, supporting an earlier decision that only one Hell's Angel had stabbed Hunter, and that the killing was done in self-defence.

record company was worried about the cover's graffiti art; *Sticky Fingers*, with its suggestive zipper-fly, was criticized for being overtly sexual; and *Their Satanic Majesties Request*, as an album name, gave ammunition to those who accused the Stones of being in some way connected with darkness, death, and evil. But through the controversy, the band kept writing hit songs and touring.

Mick Taylor left in 1975 and was replaced by Ron Wood. Later, as Jagger, Richards, and the others turned 40, there was a long inactive period when Jagger and Richards didn't speak to each other much. Wyman quit in the early '90s, tired of three decades of taking orders from Jagger and Richards. He was replaced, and the Stones kept rolling. Well into their sixties now, they're still at it.

Along with U2, they're the biggest concert draw in the rock world. They still produce new music, including 2005's *A Bigger Bang*. Each album is followed by a mammoth tour. The shows sell out stadiums all over the world.

The Stones have outlasted everyone else, and finally inherited their 1969 title: the World's Greatest Rock and Roll Band.

In Brief

Neil Young wrote "Ohio" immediately after a tragic shooting incident during a student protest at Ohio's Kent State University. Recorded by the super-group Crosby, Stills, Nash, and Young, the song was on the radio less than two weeks after the shootings. It still stands as one of rock's most potent political statements, and exemplifies the intensity and passion that have made Neil Young one of rock's most prolific, distinctive and respected song-writers and performers.

Neil Young and Crosby, Stills, & Nash
May 1970

Stephen Stills, Graham Nash, David Crosby, and Neil Young in performance.

The Band

All four of Crosby, Stills, Nash, and Young (CSNY) were talented multi-instrumentalists, but they're mainly remembered as follows:

David Crosby	★	vocals, acoustic guitar, background harmonies
Stephen Stills	★	vocals, electric guitar, keyboards
Graham Nash	★	vocals, acoustic guitar, background harmonies
Neil Young	★	electric and acoustic guitar, vocals

Crosby, Stills, Nash, and Young all wrote songs. On stage and in the studio, the band added a drummer and bass player to fill out the sound.

The Background

DAVID CROSBY, STEPHEN STILLS, GRAHAM NASH, AND NEIL YOUNG together made up the first American "supergroup," with four members who were individually famous prior to uniting. The group might never have existed if it hadn't been for a series of chance meetings, good timing, and lucky coincidences. But when they finally did get together, their talents combined to make some of the most memorable music of the late '60s.

Young spent his early childhood in Toronto, then moved with his mother to Winnipeg when his parents divorced. In his early teens, he fell in love with the music on the radio—the songs of Little Richard, Elvis Presley, and Cliff Richard and the Shadows. He taught himself to play guitar and formed a band with some high-school friends.

Young was serious enough about music that he dropped out of school to follow his dreams. By 1964, he had led his band to Toronto, but without consistent work or any record company interest, some members quit. For a frustrating year and a half, Young

Toronto, Ontario, was home to Neil Young during some of his early years as a professional musician.

had to rely on his father, Scott, a well-known journalist, for loans. He struggled, playing wherever he could.

Meanwhile, in California, Crosby had co-founded the American folk-rock group the Byrds in 1964. The Byrds had many mid-'60s hits with their distinctive jangly guitar sound and close, complex harmonies. But in 1968, Crosby left the band to launch a solo career.

Nash was an original member of the English pop band the Hollies. During the mid-'60s, the Hollies were second only to the Beatles on the British charts. Nash sang, played guitar, and wrote many of the band's best-known songs. But, like Crosby, Nash was soon interested in making more adventuresome, complex music than his band-mates wanted.

Stills, who moved around the American South during his youth, learned to play guitar, piano and drums. In the mid-'60s, he joined a New York-based band and was on tour in Canada when he met Young, whose band was on the same bill. In the spring of 1966, Stills moved to LA, looking for the right combination of musicians to inspire him. He would succeed only when he and Young again crossed paths.

Back in Canada, Young and a bass player, Bruce Palmer, decided to leave Toronto. California was the place for exciting new music, and Young had heard that Stephen Stills was in LA. They set off in Young's old black Buick hearse, driving south and west across North America.

What happened after they reached LA is one of the great lucky accidents in rock history. Young and Palmer had spent days unsuccessfully trying to track down Stills and were planning to head north to San Francisco. Stuck in a traffic jam on a busy LA freeway, Young's hearse, with distinguishing Ontario license plates, was spotted by Stills and a friend,

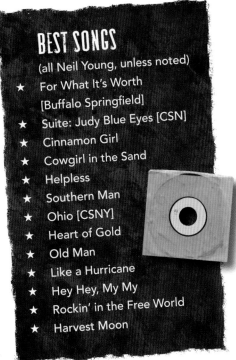

BEST SONGS

(all Neil Young, unless noted)

★ For What It's Worth [Buffalo Springfield]
★ Suite: Judy Blue Eyes [CSN]
★ Cinnamon Girl
★ Cowgirl in the Sand
★ Helpless
★ Southern Man
★ Ohio [CSNY]
★ Heart of Gold
★ Old Man
★ Like a Hurricane
★ Hey Hey, My My
★ Rockin' in the Free World
★ Harvest Moon

It was a stroke of luck that Stephen Stills recognized Neil Young's hearse among the cars of an LA traffic jam. Young's Buick was the second hearse he'd owned, but soon after joining forces with Stills, he graduated to limousines.

who were driving the other way. They turned around and flagged the hearse down.

Stills' friend, Ritchie Furay, was a musician too. Together, the four formed a band, adding drummer Dewey Martin. They called themselves Buffalo Springfield (after a kind of steamroller). Within a few months they had opened for the Byrds and had been offered a record contract. Their first album came out in early 1967 and featured original songs by Young and Stills, including Stills' antiwar hit "For What It's Worth." But Buffalo Springfield didn't last long. In 1968, the band split, partly because Young and Stills were each used to being leaders. Both were writing songs furiously, competing for control.

In that same year, Stills met Nash and Crosby when the Hollies toured the US. The three of them sat around one night playing, and they were instantly impressed with how well Nash and Crosby harmonized together. Soon after this, Nash left the Hollies to work with his new American friends.

As for Young, he spent the rest of the year writing and recording a solo album, but when it was released in January 1969, he wasn't satisfied. He was looking for a new sound, less polished and structured. He needed a group that played with lots of energy—with more instinctive feel than

With the backing band Crazy Horse, Young recorded and released his second solo album, *Everybody Knows This Is Nowhere*. Successful with fans and critics, it had all the hallmarks of every Young album to follow: raw electric-guitar rock alternating with acoustic country-folk ballads; extended lead guitar solos played in Young's passionate style; and evocative lyrics sung in his high, quavering voice.

LIVE ALBUMS AND STUDIO ALBUMS

For the most part, music is recorded in one of two ways: in a recording studio, or "live" in front of an audience.

In the studio, the producer is generally in charge. He or she can ask the musicians to re-do their parts until everyone's satisfied with the result. The producer may also record only certain instruments at first—for example, the drums, bass, and rhythm guitar—and then add lead guitar, keyboards, and vocals one at a time, layering these parts on top of what's already been done. In this way, the song is built up gradually, just as a house is built from the ground up. Some musicians, though, (Neil Young, for example) prefer to treat the studio almost like a live performance, with the whole band playing and being recorded at once, "live off the floor."

Bands frequently release live albums in addition to their studio albums. Live albums are recorded at concerts, with mobile recording equipment. They capture the excitement and spontaneity of a live performance. In front of an audience, musicians take chances, songs are extended, and the playing and singing is often more inspired. In addition, a live album shows how well the band relates to its fans, and usually features the band's best-known songs.

Some notable live albums:

★ *Before the Flood*—Bob Dylan and the Band

★ *Get Yer Ya-Ya's Out*—the Rolling Stones

★ *Live at Leeds*—the Who

★ *Live Rust*—Neil Young

technical skill. In the spring, he started jamming for fun with an LA club band called the Rockets. Danny Whitten (guitar), Billy Talbot (bass), and Ralph Molina (drums) were exactly what Young had heard in his head as the ideal sound. He renamed the band Crazy Horse and hired them as his backing band.

Meanwhile, Crosby, Stills, and Nash had formed a group and put out their first album in June 1969. Stills' songs were especially strong, particularly his seven-minute "Suite: Judy Blue Eyes," which Crosby and Nash augmented with their trademark harmony vocals. The album and its singles were major hits, and Crosby, Stills, and Nash were immediately elevated to star status.

But to tour and perform at the world's biggest gigs—like Woodstock, in the summer of 1969— Crosby, Stills, and Nash knew they needed more power onstage. They also knew that adding one more dynamic singer, guitarist, and songwriter to their lineup would strengthen the band overall, helping them live up to the reputation they'd acquired as the "American Beatles."

Stills knew they could find all these qualities in one man: his old Buffalo Springfield bandmate, Neil Young.

CSNY's music and personalities seemed to attract fans determined to hang onto the '60s values of peace, love, and togetherness, even as those values were tested by the social and political events at the end of the decade— assassinations, violent protests, and the escalation of the Vietnam War.

The Making of a Supergroup

Unlike Crosby, Stills, and Nash, Neil Young always intended to keep his solo career going while contributing to CSNY. But CSNY were very busy throughout the rest of 1969. They played the Woodstock festival and continued touring into the fall. Young only had time for occasional gigs with Crazy Horse. Throughout the year, CSNY grew more and more popular. During the winter of 1969–1970, the band recorded when not touring. Young's raw, spontaneous approach in the studio was very different from the way the others had created their first album, and this difference caused arguments. CSNY were not often in the studio all together—rather, each songwriter completed his own songs by bringing in the others as needed.

The recording sessions finished early in 1970. The resulting album,

Déjà Vu, contained some of CSNY's best-loved songs. Nash's "Teach Your Children" and Crosby's "Almost Cut My Hair" were the band's comments on the widening generation gap, and the band's rocking cover of singer-songwriter Joni Mitchell's "Woodstock" summed up much of young America's feelings about the recent festival and all it stood for. Young's strongest song was "Helpless," a sad, beautiful hymn about the impossibility of returning to the innocence of childhood.

Young spent the spring of 1970 playing with Crazy Horse, and planning a new solo album. But in May, the Kent State disaster brought state-sanctioned violence to America's university community. It was this tragedy that would pull CSNY back together to record their most enduring song.

During the Vietnam War, the American government supported South Vietnam in its fight against communist North Vietnam. Back in the US, those who opposed the war questioned the legitimacy of the South Vietnamese government in Saigon (now called Ho Chi Minh City).

THE VIETNAM WAR

The US became officially involved in the Vietnam War in 1964, and by the following year, young Americans were being sent to fight in Vietnam. Anti-war protests began almost immediately on college campuses across the US, and as the war effort escalated, so did the student protests.

Throughout 1969, President Nixon reduced the number of American troops in Vietnam, but the media continued to relay footage of the war's horrors. The protests grew, against not only the government's foreign policy, but also the mandatory military service, or "draft," that came with it.

Then, after dismissing protesters as being "bums...blowing up the campuses," President Nixon ordered American forces to move into Cambodia, which borders Vietnam. By the next day, more student protests had begun.

WHAT HAPPENED AT KENT STATE

At first the problems at Kent State were no different than at other demonstrations elsewhere. But during a weekend of protests and escalating confrontation between students and local police, the Ohio National Guard—army-trained solders with full equipment including M-1 rifles—arrived on the campus. To the students, the tough, authoritarian Guardsmen symbolized all that was wrong with America.

The students assembled for another rally on Monday morning, May 4. They believed they had a right to hold this demonstration. But just before noon, the National Guard—now 1,000 strong—addressed the crowd of about 1,500 through a bullhorn: "This assembly is unlawful. This crowd must disperse immediately. This is an order."

The crowd did not disperse. The Guardsmen readied their weapons and strapped on gas masks. They tossed tear gas canisters at the students and advanced. The demonstrators backed away, yelling and throwing rocks. Back and forth they went, until one troop of Guardsmen stood on top of a small hill on campus. With students in front and to the side of them, the Guardsmen swiftly raised their rifles, took aim, and fired.

Shots rang out for 13 seconds. Four students were killed and nine others wounded. Of the four dead, two had been involved in the protest. The others were bystanders, on their way to eat lunch after classes.

Later, official commissions and FBI investigations concluded that some blame for the incident rested on the National Guard and even on President Nixon. But they also determined that the students had been partially responsible. Many Americans agreed. The country seemed to have lost its sympathy for public demonstrations.

Terrified Kent State University students flee from the gunfire of the National Guard.

Four Shootings and a Song

The immediate impact and lasting resonance of CSNY's "Ohio" is a reflection of the tensions in the US and the political involvement of American youth at the time.

The '60s was a decade of student uprisings, especially protests against the American participation in the Vietnam War. On April 30, 1970, the US government widened the scope of the war by moving into Cambodia. The next day, antiwar protests and riots broke out at universities all over the US. This reaction was expected. But the death of four students at the Kent State University protests shocked the nation. Neil Young transformed his own sorrow and sympathy into three minutes of searing music, and his song gave many an outlet for their own grief.

Young and Crosby were in California when the shootings happened. The following day, Young saw a photograph of one student crying over another student's body. According to Crosby, Young "got out his guitar and wrote the song right there in front of me." Within 24 hours, CSNY were in the studio completing the song.

"Ohio" begins with a low, menacing electric guitar line. As the drums and bass enter, Young's piercing lead guitar climbs up high and back down again before the verse starts. The lyrics are heavy with images of the soldiers, Nixon, and the four slain students. Over a thumping, military backbeat, Young urges the listener to imagine if the dead student were a friend. There are only two short verses, but "Ohio" captures perfectly the anger

BEST ALBUMS
(all Neil Young, unless noted)

★ Crosby, Stills, and Nash (1969) [CSN]
★ Everybody Knows This Is Nowhere (1969)
★ Déjà Vu (1970) [CSNY]
★ After the Goldrush (1970)
★ Harvest (1972)
★ Tonight's the Night (1973)
★ Decade (1977) [greatest hits compilation]
★ Rust Never Sleeps (1979)
★ Ragged Glory (1990)
★ Harvest Moon (1992)

Vietnam: American troops distract themselves from the day's battles by playing music. Soldiers fighting in Vietnam—whose average age was 19—enjoyed the same electric rock and roll popular with the *anti*war culture.

and the dread of the Kent State shootings. Crosby, Stills, and Nash add rich harmony vocals to the choruses and final lines, with Crosby howling "why?" and "how many more?" as the song fades out.

For once, Young was satisfied with what happened in the studio. However, he was uneasy about profiting indirectly from the incident.

Atlantic Records rushed "Ohio" out as a single in just over a week after the shooting. With the country still grieving over the dead students, the song came stalking out of radio speakers like a ghost pointing its finger at those responsible. Many conservative stations banned "Ohio," but it was played extensively on underground FM stations and quickly became a rallying cry for people opposed to the Vietnam War and to a government that treated human lives so carelessly. "Ohio" galvanized young people across America and gave strength to further protests.

The following year CSNY released a live album, *Four Way Street.* Among some uneven material, Young's performances were the strongest; but the record showed that the group was moving in separate directions. By 1972, Young and Stills had returned to solo work. Crosby and Nash released an album together. Crosby, Stills, and Nash would continue to re-unite occasionally, as a trio, but their time as one of America's most significant bands was over. Neil Young, however, was just hitting his stride.

Since Then

In the years since 1970, Young has become a legend. He has released many albums in many styles, including folk, country, techno, rockabilly, and hard rock. He's experimented with new technologies, including filmmaking, but remained true to his approach to songwriting and recording—no frills, raw, and honest. His high voice and chunky guitar playing are instantly recognizable. He has exaggerated and made the most of his personal quirks, rather than trying to smooth them out for the public.

NEIL YOUNG'S MAIN INFLUENCES

★ Cliff Richard and the Shadows (early British rock and roll band)
★ Roy Orbison ('50s and early '60s American rock and roll singer)
★ Bob Dylan
★ The Beatles
★ the Byrds (American folk-rock band)
★ Jimi Hendrix

After the summer of 1970, there were not many more of the protest marches and sit-ins that had been so common in the previous decade. Those 13 seconds of gunfire at Kent State likely killed what was left of the political spirit of '60s America, and it seems that spirit has never recovered.

NEIL YOUNG'S MUSICAL DESCENDANTS

★ America
★ Sonic Youth
★ Soul Asylum
★ the Jayhawks
★ Blue Rodeo
★ the Cowboy Junkies
★ Nirvana
★ Pearl Jam
★ the Bottle Rockets
★ Wilco
★ Son Volt
★ Pete Droge

Young's work in different genres has inspired a wide variety of musicians. He's often referred to as "the Godfather of Grunge" because of his influence on Nirvana's Kurt Cobain and other Seattle-area musicians who adopted Young's "uniform" of plaid work shirt, jeans, and work boots, and the loud, unpolished sound he pioneered with Crazy Horse.

Young still makes records and tours with Crazy Horse. Sometimes, he does solo, "unplugged" shows and albums; and he has even occasionally reunited with Crosby, Stills, and Nash to play. The other three have continued to work, mainly with each other, but their appeal is limited mostly to older audiences trying to recapture a little of yesterday's atmosphere. Only Young has continued to write and record edgy, relevant music. Now well into his sixties, he shows no sign of slowing down.

AFTER KENT

The Kent State students didn't die entirely in vain. The public outcry about the shootings galvanized 75,000 people to march on the US capitol in Washington the weekend after. Responding to the pressure, Richard Nixon eventually met with university students to discuss their concerns about the war. Many believe these talks helped speed up the government's withdrawal from Vietnam.

In the months and years that followed, Nixon slowly reduced American involvement in Vietnam and Cambodia, bringing the soldiers home gradually, until the last men arrived back in the US in early 1973.

In Brief

Led Zeppelin is the original hard rock band. Famous for distorted electric guitars, thundering bass and drums, and soaring, passionate vocals, their distinctive sound led to the development of heavy metal years after their 1968 debut.

In late 1971, the band released its fourth album. The untitled album contains "Stairway to Heaven," still the most-requested rock song on radio stations all over the world.

Led Zeppelin

November 1971

Led Zeppelin had the same four members for the duration of their career as a group: Robert Plant, John Paul Jones, Jimmy Page, and John Bonham.

The Band

Jimmy Page ★ electric and acoustic guitars
Robert Plant ★ vocals, occasional harmonica
John Paul Jones ★ bass guitar, keyboards, mandolin, recorder
John Bonham ★ drums

The four band members co-wrote the songs, though Page was responsible for most of the music and Plant generally wrote the lyrics. Page was also the band's producer, giving Zeppelin records their unique sound.

The Background

THE INDIVIDUAL MEMBERS OF LED ZEPPELIN had each paid their dues in England's music scene for many years by the time they met. Once they combined their talents, however, they soared to the top of the music world in less than a year.

All band members started playing music early and were performing as professionals as teenagers. By the time Jimmy Page was 19, he was a studio musician hired by bands to add his talents to their recording sessions. From 1964 through 1966 Page was one of the most in-demand studio guitar players in England. Some say that he played on half of the rock and pop records recorded in London during those years, including tracks by the Rolling Stones, Van Morrison, the Kinks, Eric Clapton, and the Who.

In 1966, Page was invited to join one of England's top blues-based rock bands, the Yardbirds. He began as the bass player but later became the bandleader and lead guitarist. But by 1968, the Yardbirds were falling apart. Page wanted to keep the band going with new members. He went north to the Midlands to check out singer Robert Plant, who had been recommended by a friend.

At 19 years old, Plant had already been singing in blues bands for four years. Page walked into the nightclub and was immediately impressed. Plant was a powerful and emotional singer with great range—able to hit notes far higher than most male singers could reach. He also looked confident and cool as a front man. The two hit it off right away when then realized they shared a love of traditional rock, blues, and folk music. Page invited Plant to join his band. Plant then recommended his friend: drummer John Bonham, a former bandmate.

Bonham had been playing since he was 10 years old, when his parents encouraged their boisterous son to focus his energy on drumming. By the time he met Plant, Bonham was well known not just for his tremendous skill but also for being an unusually powerful and dominant drummer. He also had a reputation for wild behavior.

Page's band was almost complete. Calling themselves the New Yardbirds, the group began rehearsing for a previously booked tour of Scandinavia. The final change came when the Yardbirds' bassist quit to become a photographer. Page replaced him with an old friend: John Paul Jones, who had already played bass on earlier Yardbirds' studio sessions.

 John Bonham influenced a new generation of drummers with his innovative style and approach to the instrument. Seeing star swing drummer Gene Krupa on TV convinced the young Bonham that a drummer could be a loud, dynamic part of the band rather than sit unnoticed at the back of the stage. He carried this attitude into his lifestyle as well as his playing.

Since 1964, Jones had been playing on the same studio circuit as Page, contributing to thousands of recording sessions by a wide variety of musicians, including Rod Stewart, Cat Stevens, the Rolling Stones, and Donovan. But by 1968, he wanted to be more creative than strict studio work allowed, and was happy to join the New Yardbirds.

Page arranged a rehearsal for his new four-piece lineup at a small room in London's Chinatown. They jammed on familiar old songs, and, in Page's words, "it was unforgettable...so powerful...just like a thunderbolt, a lightning flash." What the four musicians shaped that day—the strong groove of the rhythm section, Page's skilful guitar work, and Plant's voice on top—had the raw energy that would launch Led Zeppelin to the top of the music world in less than a year.

The Zeppelin Takes Flight

After the Scandinavian tour, the New Yardbirds, as they were still called, played a few shows of original music at London clubs. They were then given a permanent name by the Who's drummer, Keith Moon, who joked that the group would sink like a lead balloon, or zeppelin. The band loved the image and kept the name, changing the spelling to "led" to avoid mispronunciations.

In late 1968, the band's manager, Peter Grant, helped them come up with a business plan. A bearded giant who'd previously been a professional wrestler and nightclub bouncer, Grant didn't want the band to waste time trying to win the approval of England's critics and sometimes

BEST SONGS

★ Dazed and Confused
★ Whole Lotta Love
★ Heartbreaker
★ Ramble On
★ Immigrant Song

★ Black Dog
★ Stairway to Heaven
★ When the Levee Breaks
★ Kashmir
★ Achilles Last Stand

MUSIC IN THE '70S

Until the early '70s there were only a few styles of popular music. Rock, country, folk, blues, and rhythm and blues dominated the bins at the record store. But as the '70s progressed, the popular music scene became much more fractured. Rock music, especially, split into several sub-genres.

Record companies were bigger, and so less inclined to take risks. They signed artists who could sell millions of albums rather than those who were edgy or controversial. Musicians such as Queen, Kiss, Boston, and Elton John sold millions of albums and packed sports arenas for their concerts.

Harder styles of rock became either heavy metal (examples are bands such as Black Sabbath and Judas Priest) or punk (the Ramones and the Sex Pistols). Neither style was played on the radio but both had fanatical supporters. New wave (as played by musicians such as Elvis Costello and the Cars) appeared at the end of the '70s. It was a stripped-down, simple style of rock without the pretensions of the stadium bands or the noisy socio-political rage of punk. Both punk and new wave were partly a reaction to the sanitized, corporate music put out by the major record companies and their acts.

From rhythm and blues and funk came one of the decade's most popular styles, disco. Disco featured repetitive, rhythmic songs driven by up-tempo drums, bass, keyboards, and horns. It was made for dancing, and produced a dance-club culture with its own fashions. At the other end of the spectrum was folk-rock, with confessional songwriters such as Cat Stevens and James Taylor singing introspective ballads accompanied by acoustic guitars. Jazz also began to have a greater influence on pop music.

Since then, music has become even more splintered. The categories have become harder and harder to define, and more musicians combine different styles to produce new work that's exciting but difficult to classify.

Hot colors, cool stripes, and smooth polyester were required fashion elements in the early '70s. These groovy trendsetters are dancing in the streets during an outdoor concert.

Soon after the release of *Led Zeppelin II*, the classic, riff-driven tunes "Whole Lotta Love" and "Heartbreaker" became mandatory learning for every garage-band rock guitarist.

difficult-to-please audiences. Instead, he decided that they'd first focus on succeeding in the US. He negotiated a lucrative five-year recording contract with Atlantic Records, persuading the company to sign because of Page, Plant, Jones and Bonham's individual reputations.

Led Zeppelin went into the studio, and in just 36 hours, recorded their first album. Simply called *Led Zeppelin*, it was released in January 1969 and became the standard for all hard rock albums to follow. The style was defined by loud, heavy bass and drums on the bottom, powerful, overdriven guitars in the middle, and high vocals sitting on top. The band's strong playing and Page's skills as a producer and guitarist added to the record's immediate success.

Led Zeppelin toured the US, and the crowds loved them. Onstage, Bonham and Jones were a combined rhythm powerhouse, and built a pounding, rock-solid foundation for Page's memorable guitar riffs and flashy solos. Plant became the archetypal hard rock singer. With his looks and wailing, expressive voice, he appealed to everyone—girls and women thought his long hair and hippie clothes were sexy, while many guys envied his macho confidence.

The second and third albums were even more successful than the first. Released late in 1969, *Led Zeppelin II* developed hard rock further still, emphasizing heavy, repetitive guitar lines, or "riffs," more than vocal melodies. Bonham also stood out on this album, with the definitive rock drum solo in "Moby Dick."

BEST ALBUMS

★ Led Zeppelin (1969)
★ Led Zeppelin II (1969)
★ Led Zeppelin III (1970)
★ ⚡⚖⊛Ⓘ (1971)

★ Houses of the Holy (1973)
★ Physical Graffiti (1975)
★ Early Days/Latter Days (2000)
   [greatest hits package, selected by Jimmy Page]

Late in 1970, came *Led Zeppelin III*, a record that continued with the group's signature hard rock sound while developing its more delicate acoustic side. Plant and Page wrote the songs while the band was staying at a cottage in Wales, and the music reflects their growing interest in Celtic folk tunes.

Despite a highly unusual marketing approach, both *Led Zeppelin II* and *III* reached number one on album charts in the US and Britain. Grant and the

A BIGGER CANVAS

Throughout the latter half of the '60s, many bands started seeing entire albums, rather than short, radio-friendly singles, as a better way to make a musical statement. In the '70s, two bands on the vanguard of this approach were Led Zeppelin and Pink Floyd.

Pink Floyd began in England in the mid-'60s. By 1967, they were playing psychedelic rock shows, complete with exotic sound effects and creative lighting. Their albums featured long instrumental jams, experimental studio-generated sounds, and complex lyrics.

In 1973, Pink Floyd consisted of David Gilmour, Roger Waters, Rick Wright, and Nick Mason. That year, they released *The Dark Side of the Moon*. Like Led Zeppelin's ☤ △ ⊛ ⏀, it was an epic statement that won Pink Floyd millions of new fans and solidified the band's connection with long-time aficionados. The album shot straight to

number 1 and stayed on Billboard's Top 200 chart for an unprecedented 14 years. Floyd had created a new style: a lush rock sound with dramatic arrangements and philosophical, cynical lyrics about society, politics, and alienation. More success followed with the albums *Wish You Were Here*, *Animals*, and *The Wall*.

Unlike some '70s "concept albums" that now sound dated, Pink Floyd's best work is a staple on classic "AOR" (album-oriented rock) radio stations. The band's ironic take on the post-industrial world, combined with its cool, polished sound, is still as popular and relevant today.

band believed that albums should be bought and listened to as complete song cycles, so they tried to restrict Atlantic Records from releasing individual songs as singles. Only nine Zeppelin songs were ever sold as singles throughout their entire career. The band also avoided TV appearances, preferring to reach their fans at live concerts. These decisions set the band apart from other groups.

The group's fourth album, though, was about to put Led Zeppelin on the road to being the biggest rock band in the world.

Stairway to Success

Its acoustic guitar introduction is the most famous in rock music, and its closing electric guitar solo is the one most often learned by amateur players worldwide. It consistently wins "best song of all time" in audience polls, three and a half decades after its release. Simply, "Stairway to Heaven" is, to many fans, classic rock's greatest song.

It is also the central piece on Led Zeppelin's 1971 album. Without any title or mention of the band anywhere on the original jacket, the album has been referred to as *Led Zeppelin IV* and *Untitled*. It's also known by the four strange symbols printed on the jacket's spine: 𝄢 ⚭ ⊛ ⊕ , and sometimes by the word "Zoso," the first of these symbols. But while the symbolism in

Since Led Zeppelin first released "Stairway to Heaven," other bands have covered the song. Some of the more unusual versions reinterpret the song as country-bluegrass, orchestral, reggae, or punk. The Australian comedy show, *The Money or the Gun*, featured a guest artist performing "Stairway" in each weekly episode.

the album's title and lyrics is intriguing, the music is what endures.

The album opens with "Black Dog," in which a heavy guitar-and-bass riff alternates with the howls of Plant's sexual boasting. The song also features some amazing drumming—Bonham seems to be completely out of time with the rest of the band for sections, but somehow keeps the whole thing together. "Rock and Roll" showcases some great playing by Page. The album's closing song, "When the Levee Breaks," is Zeppelin's cover of an old American blues song. The drums were recorded with Bonham playing in a stairwell in a mansion, three stories below the mikes. This drum part is often sampled on hip-hop tracks because of its heavy, pounding feel.

And then there's "Stairway to Heaven." Its instant and neverending popularity may just be because it is such an unusual rock song. The eight-minute piece begins with Page's delicate, fingerpicked acoustic guitar, followed by two recorders played in harmony by Jones. Plant enters next, tentative and thoughtful as he sings his first few lines.

Gradually, the song builds. After two minutes, Page brings in an electric guitar to match the acoustic track; a minute later the drums propel the tune forward and Plant's voice grows stronger. Finally, after more than five minutes, there's a short pause, a flourish of guitars—and then the "rock" section begins, kicked off with Page's virtuoso solo against a backing of heavy bass and drums. When Plant's voice enters again, the band is rocking, unified for the first time. It stays together as the song builds, until

LED ZEPPELIN'S MAIN INFLUENCES

- ★ Willie Dixon
- ★ Robert Johnson
- ★ Howlin' Wolf
  (American blues singer-guitarists)

- ★ Scotty Moore
- ★ James Burton
  (American rockabilly guitarists from the '50s)

- ★ Elvis Presley
  (early American rocker, an influence on Robert Plant)

- ★ Bert Jansch
  (British folk musician, an influence on Jimmy Page)

- ★ Keith Moon
  (the Who's drummer, an influence on John Bonham)

- • Ravi Shankar
  (Indian composer and sitar player)

at last the music crashes and dies, leaving Plant to sing his last words alone, one of rock music's famous final lines.

What's It All About?

And what are these words about? What is ⚙ ⚛ ⊛ Ⓘ, aside from a collection of eight great tunes? Listeners have speculated about the album's meaning since its release. The lyrics have been puzzled over because they are highly symbolic, full of obscure references—and also because Page is one of rock music's best-known fans of the occult. Although it's commonly known that Plant wrote the album's lyrics, drawing on his interest in Celtic myth, many fans speculate that the words actually have hidden occult significance, influenced by Page.

It was Page who suggested that each band member choose a symbol, or "sigil," from a German book of religious and mystical signs. These four symbols gave the fourth album its name. ⚙ ⚛ ⊛ Ⓘ: Page, Jones, Bonham, Plant. Page and Plant actually designed their own sigils.

Because of this mysticism and Page's fascination with strange religion, there have always been rumors about a connection between Led Zeppelin and devil worship. Some people believed that certain Zeppelin songs would produce hidden Satanic messages when played backwards; others thought that the band's later tragedies were the price they'd paid for selling their souls to the devil. Of course, the members themselves thought these theories were ridiculous. Plant later told an interviewer, "To me it's very sad, because 'Stairway To Heaven' was written with every best intention, and as far as reversing tapes and putting messages on the end, that's not my idea of making music."

Jimmy Page was fascinated with the Celts, an ancient people who lived in Great Britain and across most of Europe. Celtic artwork features distinctive knots and interlocking patterns.

THE TOLKIEN CONNECTION

Apart from possible occult or mystical references, the other more obvious inspiration for the ⚯ ⚭ ⚮ ⚯ album came from J.R.R. Tolkien, the British author of the fantasy trilogy *The Lord of the Rings*.

Plant was a big Tolkien fan. He even went so far as to call his dog "Strider" after a character in *The Lord of the Rings*. The Tolkien influence shows up most directly on the third song on ⚯ ⚭ ⚮ ⚯, "The Battle of Evermore." Here, Plant sings of a war between light and dark, with a queen of light, a dark lord, and "ringwraiths"—all characters taken from the famous novel.

The Lord of the Rings has been extremely popular since it was published in the mid-'50s. Led Zeppelin's association with Tolkien's fantasy world, especially on their mystical, symbolically rich fourth album, distinguished them from other rock groups of the time. Zeppelin, with their hard-driving, hard-partying image, their three-hour live shows, their symbology and spiritualism, seemed to know things their audience didn't—and when these mystical truths were suggested in the context of bone-crushing rock songs, the package was irresistible.

Regardless of the real or rumored influences, ⚯ ⚭ ⚮ ⚯, the record with no name, has sold more than 20 million copies. It is currently the fourth-bestselling album of all time.

Since Then

Of all the bands featured in this book, Led Zeppelin has arguably had the greatest impact on rock music after the late '70s. Their first four albums became models for what hard rock would sound like, and by the mid-'80s, there were countless Zeppelin clones touring and selling millions of copies of their own records in North America and Europe.

Led Zeppelin themselves lasted another nine years after releasing

STAY HAPPY WITH LAFFIN GAS

In 1973, the Arab states declared they wouldn't ship oil to any country that supported their enemy, Israel, including the US, Japan, and any country in Western Europe. For five months, gas was rationed. Many filling stations simply ran out of gas. Homeowners were asked to turn down their thermostats, gas stations were told to limit the quantity sold to each customer, and speed limits were lowered.

Though they never again created another album with as much widespread impact, or a song as popular as "Stairway to Heaven," they enjoyed many further successes throughout the '70s. Zeppelin consistently broke attendance records on tour and, in 1975, all six of their albums were in the top 200 worldwide.

They were also known for enjoying the rock-star lifestyle to the maximum. With success came excess—too much alcohol and drugs, too many parties with female fans and hangers-on. The band also spent money freely: they bought their own plane for international tours. They were further distracted from music by extensive work on their concert movie, *The Song Remains the Same*, released in 1976.

But real trouble was just around the corner. In 1976, Plant and his wife were seriously injured in a car accident. Not long after this, their young son died of a viral infection. Plant took a year off to recover from the tragedy, supported by his good friend Bonham. Around the same time, Page's problems with drug addiction grew worse. The band regrouped in 1978 to record what would be another number one album and their final studio work: *In through the Out Door*. Soon after, they played a successful "comeback show" in front of a huge audience at Britain's Knebworth Festival. Still only in their early thirties, they seemed ready to rock once more.

LED ZEPPELIN'S MUSICAL DESCENDANTS

Rolling Stone magazine claimed that "Led Zeppelin invented heavy metal, then went light-years beyond it." Like Bob Dylan and the Rolling Stones, Zeppelin had a host of imitators within a few years of their peak in popularity. Here are some of the best known:

★ Aerosmith
★ Scorpions
★ Queen
★ Heart
★ AC/DC
★ Judas Priest
★ Rush
★ Van Halen
★ Whitesnake

★ Mötley Crüe
★ Soundgarden
★ Jane's Addiction
★ the Cult
★ Guns 'n' Roses
★ Pearl Jam
★ Stone Temple Pilots
★ the Tea Party

However, the band's final tragedy hit in September 1980. They had begun rehearsing for a new tour when Bonham, a legendary drinker, died in his sleep one night, choking as a result of having drunk too much. Because the four members had been so close for so long, and because Bonham's drumming was such an important part of their sound, the others decided to disband the group. Shortly after the funeral, Peter Grant and Led Zeppelin issued a formal statement. Because of Bonham's death, the statement read, "we could not continue as we were."

MORE CLASSIC SONGS

"You Really Got Me"
The Kinks, 1964: An early rocker from a band that's often compared to the Rolling Stones and the Who. From the opening distorted guitar riff to the final choruses, this song goes flat-out. Van Halen also scored a hit with it on their 1978 debut album.

"Good Vibrations"
The Beach Boys, 1966: A long, effortlessly complex song, one of the most musically sophisticated singles ever released—but it sounds so simple! It's California surf music at its best. It also inspired the Beatles to create *Sgt. Pepper*.

"Respect"
Aretha Franklin, 1967: Although not a rock song (Franklin is known as "the Queen of Soul"), this deserves a place on any list of classic songs. Aretha's one of the strongest singers ever—male or female—and she's at her best in this cool, sassy tune.

"The Weight"
The Band, 1968: The classic campfire song, done by Bob Dylan's old backing band. With its simple, folky melody and odd cast of characters, it sounds like a mysterious piece of American history. Hard to believe it hasn't been around since the Civil War.

"(Sittin' on) the Dock of the Bay"
Otis Redding, 1968: Redding is an African-American soul singer, but his song is a "crossover"—in other words, it won an audience with white listeners, as well. A beautiful melody, with a lyric full of sadness and longing.

"Sweet Thing"

Van Morrison, 1968: A strange, shimmering song from a beautiful acoustic album called *Astral Weeks*. The song is like an impressionist painting, free of the usual shape and structure of a rock song. There are touches of jazz and Celtic music.

"Layla"

Eric Clapton, 1970: Released under Clapton's band name Derek and the Dominoes. "Layla," written for George Harrison's wife, may just be rock's most passionate love song. It rocks, driven by great guitar playing from Clapton. The Allman Brothers' Duane Allman plays slide guitar through a beautiful final instrumental section.

"Big Yellow Taxi"

Joni Mitchell, 1970: A folk-rock tune with a serious message, put across with playful irony by Mitchell. It's been adopted by environmentalists because of the lyrics, which Mitchell sings in her trademark high, beautiful voice.

"Black Magic Woman"

Santana, 1970: Great playing by Mexican guitar ace Carlos Santana over a fiesta of funky Latin percussion. This song's from Santana's album *Abraxas*, which influenced many Latin-style rock bands.

"Truckin'"

The Grateful Dead, 1970: One of America's favourite cult bands spins an autobiographical account of its trips, triumphs, and busts. The Dead are acoustic rockers, with traces of folk, blues, and country thrown into the mix.

"American Pie"

Don McLean, 1971: A decade of music history rolled into eight rocking minutes, with one of the best-loved choruses ever. McLean's tribute to the death of Buddy Holly, and to the great music that came after.

"Ziggy Stardust"

David Bowie, 1972: The key song from an outrageous concept album featuring Bowie, an androgynous rocker, adopting a sci-fi alien guise and singing tunes ranging from hard rock to ballads. The definitive "glam-rock" record and a huge influence on later groups.

"Money"

Pink Floyd, 1973: A catchy, ironic song from a massively popular band off their album *Dark Side of the Moon*—still one of the bestselling albums of all time. Floyd's music is smooth, dark, spacey, and philosophical, and has influenced many of today's bands.

SELECTED BIBLIOGRAPHY

Amburn, Ellis, *Pearl: The Obsessions and Passions of Janis Joplin* (London: Warner Books, 1994).

Burrows, Terry, ed., *ITV Visual History of the Twentieth Century* (London: Carlton Books, 1999).

Davis, Erik, *Led Zeppelin:* ⚡ ⚭ ⊛ ⓘ (New York: The Continuum International Publishing Group, Inc., 2005).

Downing, David, *A Dreamer of Pictures: Neil Young, The Man and His Music* (London: Bloomsbury, 1994).

The Bootleg Series, Vol. 4: Bob Dylan Live 1966; The "Royal Albert Hall" Concert [CD, booklet notes by Tony Glover] (Columbia, Sony Music Entertainment, 1998).

Hardy, Phil and Dave Laing, *Encyclopedia of Rock* (New York: Macmillan, 1988).

Heylin, Clinton, *Bob Dylan: The Recording Sessions 1960–1994* (New York: St. Martin's Press, 1995).

Hopkins, Jerry and Danny Sugerman, *No One Here Gets Out Alive* (New York: Warner Books, 1980).

Jennings, Peter and Todd Brewster, *The Century* (New York: Doubleday, 1998).

Joplin, Laura, *Love, Janis* (Toronto: Viking, 1992).

Loder, Kurt, interviewer: interview with Keith Richards, *Rolling Stone Twentieth Anniversary,* Nov–Dec 1987, pp. 65–67.

Logan, Nick and Bob Woffinden, *The Illustrated Encyclopedia of Rock* (London: Salamander Books Ltd., 1976).

Marcus, Greil, *Invisible Republic* (New York: Henry Holt and Company, 1997).

Miller, Jim, ed., *The Rolling Stone Illustrated History of Rock and Roll* (New York: Random House, 1976).

Pritchard, Dave and Alan Lysaght, *The Beatles: An Oral History* (Toronto: Stoddart, 1998).

Redding, Noel and Carol Appleby, *Are You Experienced: The Inside Story of the Jimi Hendrix Experience* (New York: Da Capo Press, 1996).

Shelton, Robert, *No Direction Home* (Sevenoaks, Kent: New English Library, 1986).

Sumrall, Harry, *Pioneers of Rock and Roll: 100 Artists Who Changed the Face of Rock* (New York: Billboard, 1994).

Ward, Ed and Geoffrey Stokes and Ken Tucker, *Rock of Ages: The Rolling Stone History of Rock and Roll* (New York: Simon & Schuster, 1986).

en.wikipedia.org/wiki/The_beatles

www.aboutthebeatles.com/misc_sgtpepper.html

en.wikipedia.org/wiki/Neil_Young

en.wikipedia.org/wiki/Vietnam_war

www.thewho.net/irishjack/index.html

www.westminsterinc.com/who1965/goldhawk.htm

www.led-zeppelin.com/bio.html

CITED MATERIALS

[All quotations from CCR members—band history]
Bordowitz, Hank, *Bad Moon Rising: The Unofficial History of Creedence Clearwater Revival* (New York, London: Schirmer Books; Prentice Hall International, 1998). pp. 29, 30, 32, 45, 62, 80

[Jimi Hendrix on his Woodstock version of "The Star Spangled Banner"]
Brown, Tony, *Jimi Hendrix In His Own Words* (London: Omnibus Press, 1994). pp. 33, 37

[Robert Plant's comments on hidden messages in "Stairway to Heaven"]
Considine, J.D., "Life in a Lighter Zeppelin," *Musician*, Dec. 1983, http://www.led-zeppelin.org/reference/index.php?m=int18

[George Martin's comments; Bob Dylan's comment; John Lennon's comment about growing up fast]
Hertsgaard, Mark, *A Day in the Life: The Music and Artistry of the Beatles* (New York: Delacorte Press, 1995). pp. 39, 50, 96, 265

[Bob Dylan's quotations about songwriting and about "Like a Rolling Stone"]
Heylin, Clinton, *Bob Dylan: Behind the Shades* (New York: Summit Books, 1991). pp. 67, 106, 131

[Comments from Mike Bloomfield, Eric Clapton, the *L.A. Times* music reviewer; Hendrix's comments about the establishment]
Hopkins, Jerry, *The Jimi Hendrix Experience* (London: Plexus, 1996). pp. 31, 81, 90, 118, 171

[Jimi Hendrix, on the Dick Cavett show]
en.wikipedia.org/wiki/Jimi_Hendrix#1970

[Ray Manzarek on his life goal]
Manzarek, Ray, *Light My Fire: My Life with the Doors* (New York: G.P. Putnam's Sons, 1998). p. 97

[Pete Townshend, John Entwistle on their early history]
Marsh, Dave, *Before I Get Old: The Story of the Who* (New York: St. Martin's Press, 1983). pp.18, 28

[Altamont concert stage dialogue]
Maysles, Albert and David Maysles and Charlotte Zwerin, dir., *Gimme Shelter* (Abkco Studios, 1992).

[Quotations from David Crosby, Neil Young about "Ohio"]
McDonough, Jimmy, *Shakey* (Toronto: Random House, 2002). pp. 345, 346

[Bob Dylan's comments, "Royal Albert Hall" concert]
Scorsese, Martin, dir., *No Direction Home* (Paramount, 2005).

[Kent State sidebar: quotation from National Guard]
Viorst, Milton, *Fire in the Streets: America in the 1960s* (New York: Simon and Schuster, 1979). p. 535

[Quotation from Jimmy Page about first band rehearsal; official statement disbanding the group]
Wall, Mick, "Crash Landing (Led Zeppelin's Last Days)," *Guitar World*, February 2006. pp. 88, 159

[Keith Moon quotation]
Welch, Chris, *Teenage Wasteland: the Early Who* (Chessington, Surrey: Castle Communications, 1995). p. 19

[Bruce Springsteen on Bob Dylan]
en.wikipedia.org/wiki/Like_a_Rolling_Stone

FURTHER READING

Brackett, Nathan and Christian Hoard, *The New Rolling Stone Album Guide* (New York: Fireside, 2004).

Crampton, Luke and Dafydd Rees, *Rock and Roll Year By Year* (New York: DK Publishing, 2005).

George-Warren, Holly and Patricia Romanowski and Jon Pareles, ed., *The Rolling Stone Encyclopedia of Rock & Roll* (New York: Fireside, 2001).

Life Magazine ed., *LIFE Rock and Roll at 50: A History in Pictures* (New York: Life Books, 2002).

INDEX

PHOTO CREDITS

cover, title page, 11, 12, 14, 24, 28, 29, 47, 60, 71 (top), 81 (top), 84, 99, 105, 113, 120 (bottom), 127, 136: © istockphoto.com

3, 5, 6, 9 (bottom), 10, 13, 18, 23, 32–33, 48, 54, 55, 61, 74, 81 (bottom), 98, 101 (top), 102, 109 (bottom), 125, 128, 130, 135, 142: © US National Archives and Records Administration

4 (l to r): © istockphoto.com/Jeff Griffin; © istockphoto.com; © istockphoto.com/Nathan Watkins

7, 26, 37, 44, 65, 76, 79, 91, 93, 131, 137: © Michael Ochs Archives.com

8, 22, 38, 52, 66, 80, 94, 108, 120 (top), 132: © istockphoto.com/Dan Hauser

9 (top): © istockphoto.com/Tomaz Levstek

15, 30, 45, 59, 73, 89, 101 (bottom), 115, 121, 134: © istockphoto.com/Stephanie Asher

17, 35, 49, 63, 75 (bottom), 90, 103, 116, 129 (top), 139: © istockphoto.com/Gertjan Hooijer

19, 50, 64, 77, 92, 106, 118, 143: © istockphoto.com/Ayaaz Rattansi

21: © Cummings Archives/Redferns

25: © GAB Archives/Redferns

27: © istockphoto.com/Gerrit Polder

31: © istockphoto.com/Nathan Fultz

36: © istockphoto.com/Pilar Echeverria

39: © istockphoto.com/Carrie Winegarden

40: © Virginia Turbett/Redferns

41: © istockphoto.com/Matthias Weinrich

42: © Graham Lowe/Redferns

43: © istockphoto.com/ Mike Pettifer

46: © istockphoto.com/Camilio Jimenez

51: © Gunter Zint/Redferns

53: © istockphoto.com/Ryan Klos

57: © istockphoto.com/Victor Burnside

58: © istockphoto.com/Mark Joyce

ABOUT THE AUTHOR

MIKE TAUGHT HIMSELF GUITAR AT AGE 15 and was soon performing with bands at local venues. He started writing songs in his teens—very badly at first, but gradually improving. After a few years, he began recording demo tapes, then made three albums of original music, featuring a number of different bands he'd formed and folded over the years.

He began writing prose around 10 years ago so that he could write more than the restrictions of a four-minute song allowed. He has written an adult novel and the young adult novel, *Resurrection Blues*.

On the music front, Mike continues to play regularly with his band, the Circumstantialists. He lives with his family in Toronto, Ontario.